MOUNT'S BAY

Douglas Williams

Bossiney Books

**To my daughters
Karen and Jakki**

First published in 1984
by Bossiney Books
St Teath, Bodmin, Cornwall
Designed, printed and bound in Great Britain by
A. Wheaton & Co. Ltd, Exeter

© Douglas Williams 1984
ISBN 0 906456 88 6

ABOUT THE AUTHOR—
AND THE BOOK

Douglas Williams, who has always lived and worked in West Cornwall, has his home at Newlyn, the fishing town where he was born.

Married, with two daughters, he has been a local journalist for over thirty years, and knows Mount's Bay, its places and its people, from his own personal involvement in the area and from his family background here.

The imposing scene at the Cornish Gorsedd, with the author in the foreground.

Music and drama are among his leisure interests, and he has sung with operatic and choral societies throughout Cornwall. The Rotary Club movement and the Methodist Church, also play an important part in his life. A Bard of the Cornish Gorsedd, his Bardic name sums up his interests, 'Voice and Pen'.

In his debut for Bossiney, Douglas Williams draws skilfully on his three decades in newspapers. 'Through the post-war years, as a journalist, I have learned of many of its triumphs and tragedies, interviewed its heroes and visited the towns and villages. Here, in writing of its special appeal, I have *often* let the people of Mount's Bay tell its story in their individual way.'

This personal approach and a magnificent harvest of old photographs combine to prove that Land's End to The Lizard is indeed 'rich in its modern tapestry and in its antiquities'.

A book which is destined to delight Cornish men and women at home and abroad—and visitors wanting to know more about this magical corner of Cornwall.

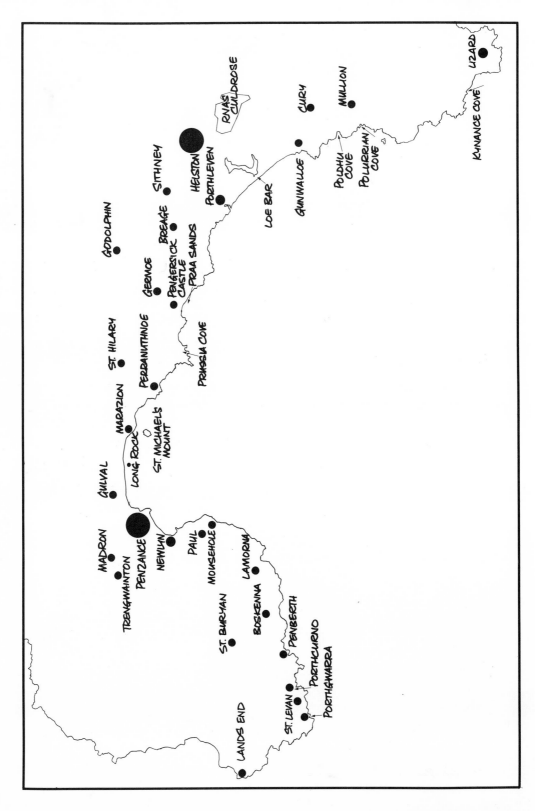

LIZARD

KYNANCE COVE

CURY

MULLION

RNAS
CULDROSE

POLDHU
COVE

POLURRIAN
COVE

HELSTON

PORTHLEVEN

SITHNEY

BREAGE

LOE BAR

GUNWALLOE

GODOLPHIN

GERMOE

PENGERSICK
CASTLE

PRAA SANDS

ST. HILARY

PERRANUTHNOE

PRUSSIA COVE

MARAZION

LONG ROCK

ST. MICHAEL'S
MOUNT

GULVAL

MADRON

PENZANCE

TRENGWAINTON

NEWLYN

PAUL

MOUSEHOLE

LAMORNA

ST. BURYAN

BOSKENNA

PENBERTH

PORTHCURNO

PORTHGWARRA

LANDS END

ST. LEVAN

Contents

Introduction

Let me tell you about Mount's Bay, its places and its people and take you to almost every corner of this magical part of England. Land's End to The Lizard is rich in its modern tapestry and in its antiquities.

It leads in communications as it once did in mining. It leads in tourism, with St Michael's Mount admired as much today as it was by those early Christian pilgrims. It leads with its fishing and its horticulture. It leads in heroism—as it has always done.

Mount's Bay changes its mood almost every day. Fiercely blue and inviting, grey-black and forbidding, whipped white and all-threatening, blue-green and entreating: the sea is in command. Whatever the wind some corner finds protection, but it can always be a great 'maritime trap', as the saga of wreck and rescue will show. Guarded by the Mount,

Guarded by St Michael's Mount (*right*) **the bay has been a haven for fishing fleets down the centuries.**

it has been a haven for fishing fleets and shipping down the centuries.

The mildness of its climate has brought a beauty and variety to the shores of the bay that have no equal in the county. It has reared a people whose independence and loyalty have been reflected in their lives.

Through the post-war years, as a journalist, I have learned of many of its triumphs and tragedies, interviewed its heroes and visited the towns and villages. Here, in writing of its special appeal, I have often let the people of Mount's Bay tell its story in their individual way.

A quiet summer corner (*right*) . . . the unbridled storms of winter (at Lamorna above) . . . Mount's Bay has many moods.

1

History All Around Us

Land's End to Lizard Light, the most westerly and southerly points of Cornwall, enclose a bay as majestic as any in Europe. Brilliant and welcoming, yet quixotic and sometimes treacherous, the seas and shore have more moods than there are Cornish Saints.

A clear moonlit night, the blue, green and gold day of summer sun, the sweeping un-bridled storms of winter, are all part of the kaleidoscope pattern of Mount's Bay.

Its arms embrace a landscape with a wealth of history and legend. The Mount is the focal point, yet the towns and villages that seem almost to face towards it in a crescent of homage have their own special claims.

The miles of beaches at Praa Sands and

'Only in the past 130 years has the railway link to Penzance and the invention of the motor-car made Mount's Bay accessible to all.' *Below*: This 3-ton Milnes-Daimler 20 h.p., pictured in 1904, was the first double-decker bus run by the GWR from Marazion through Penzance to Newlyn. *Below left*: Mullion Cove—one of the little coves 'carved into sheltered corners'.

Porthcurno, Porthchapel and Perranuthnoe, Marazion and Kynance. The coves from Porthgwarra to Gunwalloe, the cliff walks from Mousehole to Lamorna, from Penrose Woods to The Lizard, from Land's End to Penberth. This scenic path takes in almost the whole bay.

Land's End may have been a 'magnet' for thousands of years, but only in the past 130 has the railway link to Penzance, and the invention of the motor car, made it accessible to all. Those raw giant cliffs, pillars of granite, unyielding against the Atlantic, have been witness to the arrival of the first settlers from Europe and then the Celts, and to invasions from the Vikings to the Spaniards. Beneath the feet of the tourists in this peninsula is more evidence of ancient progress than in any other part of the county.

Formed millions of years ago, and carved by the sea, wind and rain, the jagged rocks throw up a wonder of designs, from 'Armed Knight' to 'Dr Syntax's Head', at the real end of the land. A mile offshore, with its new helicopter landing pad on top, the Longships Lighthouse, built in 1875, spears the air.

The great seas and cruel cliffs have two other land-based sentinels. At The Lizard the

Bill Harvey standing by his boat, the *Alpha*, (*below*) at Porthgwarra in 1903 and (*right*) hanging up skate in the tunnel.

The Logan Rock at Treen, near Porthcurno, where once guides showed visitors the magic of the rocking stone.

present lighthouse was built in 1752 with its signal a white flash every three seconds that can be seen clearly across the bay. At Tater-du, between Lamorna and Porthcurno, an unmanned light controlled from Penzance was installed a few years ago and opened by the then Duke of Gloucester, as Master of Trinity House. I remember the day well, as the Land Rover slowly brought the Royal guest down the very steep slope. Its construction followed local outcry after the tragic loss of French and Belgian fishing boats.

The little coves of Penberth and Porthgwarra, carved into sheltered corners, retain their fishing tradition, with mackerel and shellfish boats tightly moored against the waves that sweep up the slipways towards

clusters of granite cottages. That tunnel, carved out of the Porthgwarra rock, is a photographer's delight.

Porthcurno, the holidaymakers' dream, is famed for its Minack Theatre and Cable and Wireless training college. Nearby stands Treen Dinas, the first-century BC cliff castle, and the eighty-ton Logan Rock, now more celebrated for having been dislodged by young naval officer Lieutenant Goldsmith in 1824 than for its ancient 'rocking' attractions. His action ruined the business for the guides of Treen!

An artist's view of Lamorna Cove by the valley's most celebrated painter, S. J. Lamorna Birch. *Below left*: **Bosava Mill at Lamorna.**

It has been an active century for Lamorna, with the cove now under new ownership. An important time was the arrival of artist Lamorna Birch who loved the place so much that he made it part of his name. Alfred Munnings also lived here for a time. Stanhope Forbes's painting of the 'Quarry Team' hauling the granite, captured the work of those days, and huge piles of rock remain like a giant's heap of bricks. When the granite was no longer taken by sea from the cove, it was pulled to Penzance on wagons by horses, and was in great demand for its quality. It was used in the building of London's Embankment and the Wolf Rock Lighthouse. Over the years Good Friday became a gentle day out for local people, but in recent times the

occasion has degenerated into problems from youths with drink and violence, unbecoming to this lovely corner. None has lived in this lovely flower valley longer than the Hosking family who can trace their 'Lamorna connection' back to the fourteenth century.

The old name of Porth Enys—island port—is still in use in Mousehole, with its harbour mouth blocked in winter by the huge timber beams or 'baulks' to keep out the seas. There was once a hermit's cave on St Clement's Isle, and centuries ago it was the busiest of harbours in the bay. Even in 1850 there were almost a thousand people engaged in the fishing industry.

The old part of the south pier dates back to 400 AD. Today the harbour is almost empty of working boats, but the village has retained its character. More than in most Mount's Bay villages the tourist has taken

Above: **The Keigwin Arms at Mousehole in the 1880s.**
Below: **Outside the Ship Inn with a crowded harbour.**

over, with many holiday homes in the narrow streets, yet it has not been spoiled by over-development.

Sacked by the Spaniards in 1595, with the Keigwin Arms the only surviving building from those times, Mousehole is today known world-wide as the home of those gallant eight men of the Penlee lifeboat, who died at Christmas 1981 in attempting to save those on the coaster *Union Star*.

Newlyn takes pride in being a successful working port. The visit by the Queen in November 1980 to open the new £1.3 million harbour development and new pier, put the seal on progress that has taken the annual value of fish landings to well over £5 million a year. The 43-acre harbour is often as crowded as at the turn of the century, following the building of the long north and south arms, when it was the greatest mackerel port in the country.

The shelter of Gwavas Lake has not always brought calm on shore. There were 'riots' by the fishermen of Porthleven, Newlyn, Mousehole, and St Ives here in 1896, when the economic crisis caused by 'foreigners' from East Country ports fishing on Sundays—and getting the best of the Newlyn market on Mondays—boiled over into violence. In 1937 local men travelled from the harbour to the Thames in the longliner *Rosebud* in a bid to save their homes from destruction by planners.

As well as its artistic heritage the port's

Reflected glory: a Newlyn harbour scene before much development took place.

claim to fame is also in the Ordnance Tidal Observatory, close to the lighthouse, from which the datum for all ordnance maps in the British Isles is determined.

Penzance is the centre of Penwith, economically and now administratively, with the District Council headquarters based here. Granted a Charter by James I in 1614 and then acknowledged as a Coinage Town by Charles II, it grew swiftly ahead of its local rivals. It has the qualities of an old town without suffering the ravages of tourism: perhaps the lack of a long sandy beach has helped.

Unlike so many Cornish towns it has not been dependent on one industry, and remains the market town of the peninsula. There is fishing centred at its harbour, a dry dock and repair yard nearby, and the ferry *Scillonian* keeps the sea link with the Isles of Scilly twenty-five miles away. The rail terminus and the heliport make the town a strategic centre for travel.

As the hub of the farming area it has its Tuesday market. The Morrab and Penlee Gardens are of great beauty, and there are Regency and Georgian town houses to be seen in Chapel Street. The name Penzance means 'Holy Headland' but there is no trace of the old St Anthony Chapel, nor of any buildings before the Spanish invasion. From the bathing pool to Newlyn stretches an unbroken promenade and beach walk supreme in its panorama.

A lifeboat was based here (1865–1913) before the move to Penlee, but long before then Penzance had a tougher time from pirates from France, Turkey and Algeria, more sinister than Gilbert and Sullivan could imagine. Today the Pirates play Rugby!

'Pilchards and cream, tin in the stream' helped Penzance to prosperity as a port, and as it rose, neighbouring Marazion, that had earlier grown through its link with the Mount, declined in importance. It was in 1595 that it was granted its Charter by Elizabeth I, and for over 300 years had its Mayor. After losing this status in 1886, it again had a

Newlyn fishermen gazing at Big Ben with their MP, Alec Beechman, in 1937, when protesting at clearance plans for their harbour-front homes.

Mayor in 1974 in the reign of the second Elizabeth. The original Charter is still preserved and so are the ancient small maces, the large ceremonial pair of 1768 and many other historic items.

Marazion was a busy trading centre, had its own Mid-Lent and Michaelmas fairs, and although the rail station closed in the 1960s, a new development came in 1982 with the opening of a £3.8 million bypass.

Along the coast are many places to hold the interest. There is the late eighteenth-century Acton Castle, the rocky inlets of Prussia and Bessy's coves with Porth-en-Alls house, for many years host to classical music-making. There is the sweep of beaches, the caravan parks, the hamlet of Perranuthnoe, the medieval Pengersick Castle towards Rinsey Head with its old engine house.

This was mining country but the discovery of huge quantities of tin in Malaya and Australia in the 1870s contributed to a rapid decline in the Cornish industry. When copper was found in Africa and the United States, when gold and silver mines opened up around

Above: **A stormy day off Penzance promenade on the Newlyn route 100 years ago.** *Below*: **A more tranquil view looking towards Newlyn.**

A quiet day in Marazion about 1919 disturbed only by motorcycle and sidecar outside the Godolphin Arms.

the globe, there was a mass exodus of Cornish 'Cousin Jacks' searching for work.

Porthleven is another working port, proud of its boat-building and fishing industries. The first harbour was built here in 1818, but a storm destroyed it only six years later. It was rebuilt the following year. Harvey and Co. had a long-lasting interest from 1855, and built lock gates to the inner harbour to halt the power of the south-west gales. Since the war there have been steady efforts to build prosperity.

The village had its own lifeboat (1863–1929) and before that, in 1824, local men William Rowe and John Freend of Gunwalloe received the first silver medals from the RNLI for their part in the rescue of the crew from the brigantine *Olive* wrecked beneath Halzephron Cliff.

Cornwall's biggest freshwater lake, Loe

Pool, is close at hand. Legend claims it as the scene where the dying King Arthur's sword Excalibur was thrown by Sir Bedivere. With its River Cober and the Penrose woodlands it is a delightful place. The long Loe Bar of shingle divides the pool from the sea. It was here that HMS *Anson* was wrecked in 1807.

The Furry Dance and the parish church at Helston are described in another chapter, but there are many other features to admire in this town: the fine collections at the museum, once the market house, near the Guildhall—make a point of seeing the huge cider press—with the cannon from the *Anson* outside; the Blue Anchor Inn with its own 'spingo' brew; the splendid Angel Hotel in the main street— once the town house of the Godolphin family; and the ornate monument at the bottom of Coinagehall Street.

What other town has a supply of running water on either side of its main street, 'the kennels'? Helston was granted its Charter in 1201—the second in the country—and was a Stannary town during the reign of Edward I, where the local tin was assayed and stamped. The poet Coleridge's son was headmaster of the former Grammar School, and Charles Kingsley was a pupil. The town has many Regency houses, quiet lanes and gardens. Much of its economic life today rests on RNAS Culdrose, but it retains a flourishing Monday market.

The small thatched 'Toy Cottage' at Gunwalloe, on the way to Church Cove, was the home of author Sir Compton MacKenzie early this century. A fine stretch of beach to Loe Bar, a church tucked into the sand and rock, and a fishing cove are here.

For 200 years the treasure of Dollar Cove has remained an exciting enigma. Time and again there have been dreams of uncovering this tantalising hoard, only for the ever-shifting sands and rolling seas of Gunwalloe

to win the struggle. The silver dollars have come into Church Cove since an unknown vessel struck the Castle Mount rock. According to legend, her cargo of gold or pieces of silver spilled into a gully. Many attempts have been made to find it, varying from building a dam, digging a tunnel, using a dredger, to the efforts in recent years of that remarkable Cornishman, Roland Morris.

Botanists find a range of rare Cornish flowers at Goonhilly Downs and geologists look for the green serpentine. Gorse abounds, and early in summer it is a rich and open scented plain. Once it was a forest where wild animals roamed.

The accessible Poldhu Cove, with its golden sand and echoes of Marconi's triumph, leads on to his granite obelisk and to Polurrian Cove. Mullion harbour, with its sturdy pier and unique vista, was once a busy fishing port. Here were some of the cleverest pilchard men and later crab and lobster experts, who had to contend with the wildest of

Did you ever see so many fishing boats in Porthleven harbour? The scene in the 1890s.

weather. It had its own lifeboat from 1867–1909 and that stout-hearted tradition lives on at 'Porth Mellin'.

Much of the coast here is the property of the National Trust, a twentieth-century guardian. No-one can resist Kynance Cove, with its dramatic serpentine colours and caves, its giant rocks. Try to be there just after low tide when the Devil's Bellows blow with sea and spray. Just offshore are Gull Rock and Asparagus Island. The Trust has achieved much in its bid to protect the clifftop from erosion by thousands of feet, summer after summer, and in maintaining the coastal path which stretches for miles with its hardy flowers.

Wendron Street, Helston...Bob Fitzsimmons, the heavyweight champion of the world, was born here.

The Lizard, 'home of serpentine', with its craftsmen turning the rock into anything from lighthouse to ashtray, is a village and head-land sought by hundreds of thousands of tourists...and given a wide berth by wary mariners. Its coast is legend, particularly The Manacles and Black Head: little wonder a coal-fire lighthouse was kept burning from about 1620 to warn seamen. The present one has a twenty-mile range.

'Holy Palace' is the meaning of The Lizard, this tip of England, and the thatched cottages in Landewednack Churchtown, provide a charming note on which to end this sweep of the bay.

The churches of Mount's Bay have a special chapter...but may I advise the visitor to draw up his or her own special list of favourite coastal pubs. They have a person-ality of their own from the 'First and Last' to the 'Old Inn'.

Left: **Steeple Rock at Kynance in the early 1900s.**
Below: **A peaceful scene off Mullion in June 1908, pictured by Herbert Hughes.**

2

Of Castles and Kings

For thousands of years St Michael's Mount was the centre of religious, commercial and military life around Mount's Bay, just as today it is the crowning glory of the National Trust.

The pilgrims and the soldiers are replaced by the tourists. In the summer of 1983 almost 180,000 helped to make it one of the greatest attractions, the present and fourth Lord St Levan told me.

That a great sea flood of around 3000 BC turned it into an island at high tide, was one starting point in its history. 'And there can be no possible doubt,' he continued, 'that it was the island of Ictis near Belerion—the Land's End—from where tin was exported to the Mediterranean in the first century BC.

'This was the hill where they worshipped the sun, and there was a Celtic monastery here before the grant of the Mount by Edward the Confessor in the eleventh century to the Abbey of Mont St Michel in Normandy.

'One day we may find that monastery somewhere, perhaps near the Holy Rock on which St Michael appeared to the fishermen in 495 AD.'

The Cornish 'Prayer book' rebellion of 1549 is linked to the Mount in the words of the county's anthem:

If London's Tower were Michael's Hold,
We'd set Trelawny Free.

There are so many links between the history of the Mount and Royalty. The most colourful ceremony I can recall enjoying was on a summer day in 1977, when the young Prince Richard, Duke of Gloucester, visited as Grand Prior of the Order of St John of Jerusalem. There was a parade in splendid robes and the dedication service in the chapel.

It must have been a thrilling day when the Prince of Wales, later Charles II, lodged here during his escape to the Isles of Scilly in 1646, giving his name to the 'King Charles Room'. It was the same year that the Mount was surrendered to Parliamentary troops by Sir Arthur Basset.

That skilled Pretender, Perkin Warbeck, who claimed to be Duke of York, the younger of the two Princes in the Tower, had stayed there 150 years earlier, after landing at Sennen and raising his standard at Penzance. He left his faithful wife, Lady Catherine, here...and went on to his death.

The visit in 1846 of the young Queen Victoria and Prince Albert—he played the organ—is marked by an imprint of her foot on the steps where she landed from the Royal barge. A guide told me that this is a favourite feature for the tourist, while children love to see the dungeon under the chapel, hear the story of Jack the Giant Killer, and see the well halfway up the hill where Cormoran fell.

There is a charming 'Princess Room' where

Alexandra, then Princess of Wales, stayed when her husband, later King Edward VII, went on to the Isles of Scilly for a few days. I recall the visit of the Queen Mother in May 1967 on the Royal Yacht *Britannia*, especially because of her cheerfulness in the freezing weather. The Mount had one of its rare days covered in snow, but she came to lunch after calling at Penzance, and smiling despite the bitterly cold trips by sea and road.

Princess Margaret, another Royal name in

A scene from the past at St Michael's Mount.

the 'Visitors' Book' shown to me by Lord St Levan, came in 1949, and the newest Princess Alexandra in 1960. The signature 'Edward' appears in 1953, the young Duke of Kent, who had as his tutor at Eton the Hon. Giles St Aubyn, the younger brother of the present Lord.

The military tradition has been maintained. The 2nd Lord, who died in 1940, commanded the Grenadier Guards and there are spears from the Sudan battles of 1884 to prove his valour. The present Lord's father always modest and courteous, served in the Guards in the First World War, and was twice

Above: **Lord St Levan inspects a Guard of Honour, formed by the Grenadier Guards, on the Mount prior to World War II.**

Below: **St Michael's Mount boatmen wearing their eighteenth-century livery.**

wounded in France. His helmet, complete with bullet hole, is on show beside the spears.

His three sons served in the Second World War: the 4th Lord with the Royal Navy where he was awarded the DSC; the Hon. Piers St Aubyn received the MC, being dropped as a parachutist with the First Airborne Division in the battle of Arnhem—his beret is on display; and the Hon. Giles St Aubyn, who saw war service on HMS *Renown*, has been recently awarded the MVO. There is another link, with the marriage of the 4th Lord to Susan, the younger daughter of Major General Sir John Kennedy GCMG, for he was Director of Military Operations during the last war, and later Governor of Southern Rhodesia.

The Mount was the 'Cornish Tower of London' for the Duke of Hamilton, who was sent there as a prisoner during the Civil War. It was still the most isolated of places when Colonel John St Aubyn, a Parliamentary leader and the last military Governor, bought it a few years later.

Once a very familiar scene on Marazion beach, before the advent of tractor and chemical fertilisers—the carts are loaded with seaweed.

There have been romantic and remarkable personalities down the St Aubyn centuries since Charles II created the first of five baronets, all called Sir John St Aubyn. Many were Members of Parliament, and it was said of the 3rd Baronet by Walpole, when describing the Opposition: 'All these men have their price, except the little Cornish Baronet.' They were all Radical Liberals and minor gentry.

The 5th, a great collector of works of art, had fifteen illegitimate children...and hid in the big open chimney when creditors arrived! He married his second mistress Juliana Vinicombe of Marazion in 1882 and he was succeeded by his eldest illegitimate son, James, when he died seventeen years later.

Family pride was restored in 1866 when the fourth illegitimate son Edward, who inherited the Mount when brother James died in 1862, was created a Baronet. A peerage was granted in 1887 to Sir John, an MP for almost thirty years, and he became first Lord St Levan.

The walls of the castle are covered with souvenirs of history and a magnificent collection of portraits. It is a 'John Opie Museum' but it is also a home. 'People like to know that it is a family home, with the family still living here,' remarked Lord St Levan. They are also fascinated by the link with Mont St Michel, by the architecture and by the geology.

Since succeeding to the title in 1978, Lord St Levan, with the National Trust, has done an immense amount of work in restoring and repairing to make the whole castle gleam. The future planning goes on, with the knowledge of continuity in the family of love for this island home.

A cable tramway, cut through granite, carries goods to the house from the harbour below, and the latest major scheme has improved the level of the granite stones along part of the causeway. Those who have travelled by Land Rover along that narrow path at low water will need no reminding

The spectacular Victorian wing, was designed by Hon. Piers St Aubyn and built in 1873-8, and today another Piers is the heir to the title. His son, James, also loves the Mount, and now there is a third generation to continue the line, Hugh.

'We have this intention to retain the Mount as long as we can as a family home, and also to keep it open for the public,' remarked the 4th Lord. The 'Cornish charity days' are now a summer highlight, with £10,000 raised in 1983.

'I am a great believer that the public should be shown something that is still alive. This is not a dead museum, and we use all the rooms when we can,' he commented.

A view of Penzance from Castle Horneck around 1834-5.

The islanders have a Christmas party here, and the splendid Chevy Chase room is today used for special dinner parties. It was originally the refectory of the monastery, with its twelfth-century walls. On one wall is the 1660 family St Aubyn coat of arms and facing it the Royal one to celebrate the restoration of King Charles II.

Here also can be seen the medieval stained-glass windows, brought from Holland in the eighteenth century. These intrigued Prime Minister, Mrs Margaret Thatcher, and her husband, when they visited some years ago, for a representation of Hell shows that they were all ladies there, while the men—with one exception—were in Heaven!

Look around and there are many other unexpected touches. There is the Egyptian mummified cat of 2000 BC, and the 'absolutely accurate' model of the Mount made from champagne corks by Henry Lee, butler

With their backs to the Mount, women pick the
early spring flowers. *Below*: packing blooms at Mr
Sampson Hosking's flower farm at Lamorna in 1938.
Today, most flowers leave Cornwall in the bud.

Part of the courtyard of Godolphin Manor.

to the 2nd Lord. In the chapel is a fifteenth-century carving of St John the Baptist's head on a charger—where did it come from? Down in the dungeon hidden underneath the choir stalls was discovered a seven-foot skeleton—was it the legendary giant Cormoran?

The Schofield family have brought Cornish history alive with the restoration of Godolphin House, and revived the stories and legends with which this proud building is associated.

It was in 1937 that Mr Sydney Schofield bought this ancient home on the lower slopes of Godolphin Hill, and from this time to his death in 1983, devoted much of his life to it. Prince Charles, later Charles II, is reputed to have slept here while escaping to the Isles of Scilly—there is still a King's Room—where Sir Francis Godolphin was Governor.

William Godolphin received his knighthood from Henry VIII, and his nephew has his place in local history as the Cornish leader who faced the Spaniards when they raided Mount's Bay in 1595.

Sidney, 1st Earl Godolphin, was the most illustrious of them all. He was Lord High Treasurer to Queen Anne, but his title came to an end within seventy years, with the link coming to the Duke of Leeds, through marriage, until fairly recent times.

The great Sidney lies in Westminster Abbey, but his wife Margaret in Breage Parish Church. She came to Cornwall only on her death, in giving birth to their only son, and there was a fourteen day procession by coach from London costing about £1,000.

The body was rested at Godolphin and then taken to church. Her death has led to legends of the 'Lady in White', and Mrs Mary

The dining room at Godolphin Manor.

Schofield told me of these as we toured the restored and beautified house, much of which dates from about 1475.

One of the most remarkable sightings was by her daughter Elizabeth, when she was only three and was frightened by a 'white lady with long black curls who blew me a kiss'. She disappeared through what is now a cupboard, but was later learned to have been the door through to a wing that had been pulled down.

Another person saw a man-at-arms in the King's Room, yet another saw a funeral procession going up the walk that Margaret Godolphin would have passed along. Mrs Schofield herself has seen a 'King Charles' figure looking out of the middle window in the King's Room while she sat in the dining room. She saw him half a dozen times, she told me.

Legend has it that the beautiful 'Lady in White' has been seen on a terrace, and there is also the story of a walled-up room in which it was claimed a monk had been seen baptising an infant.

In front of the house there is a red mark on the paving stones, and although Mr Schofield once scrubbed it clean the blood-coloured stain remains. A messenger is thought to have been shot here—there are slits for guns at each end of this entrance—but it might well be the result of copper or tin deposits finding their way up through the earth.

My favourite story concerns the 2 February Candlemas custom by the Reeve of the Manor of Lambourne, acting for the St

Aubyn family of Pencarrow who had won part of the Godolphin Manor estate in a wager. In a custom maintained until the Duke of Leeds sold the House in 1921, a representative kept the claim alive by knocking at the door and declaring: 'Oyez, Oyez, Oyez. Here come I...to demand my Lord's dues, eight groats and a penny in money, a loaf, a cheese, a collar of brawn and a jack of the best ale in the house.'

The last to carry out the tradition was the coachman at Clowance, but I believe Mrs Schofield would like to have this re-enacted each year. What a splendid idea.

Close to a caravan site, and a busy holiday centre, the sixteenth-century Pengersick

Right: **Pengersick Castle—an unexpected delight—built in 1535 close to Praa Sands** (*below*).

Castle catches the unsuspecting traveller by surprise.

There is nothing quite like it in Cornwall: it has a character and a history all its own. Fortunately the past sixty years have seen a great deal of work and care put into its restoration and repair, and today it is 'home' for Mr and Mrs A. H. Evans who bought it some ten years ago, and came in retirement from Wiltshire.

What remains of the castle are the rooms of the original tower, with its magnificent circling granite staircase of 65 steps. At ground level is the gun room, with its defensive six-gun ports for small cannon.

At a period when there was little armament available, this was very well fortified. Built in 1535 close to Praa Sands, it was derelict by the end of the seventeenth century and then became a farm building and barn...with horses stabled in the gun room.

It ended by belonging to the Duke of

Leeds but then a Mr Evans, no relation to the present owner, bought it in the 1920s, re-roofed it and turned it into a house for the first time for over 200 years.

He did a great deal of restoration, and repairs were continued by Mr John Schofield, continuing a family tradition from Godolphin House where his father, Mr Sydney Schofield, was doing such rewarding work.

John had foresight and expertise, sharing the concern of many in the county at the loss of Cornwall's old buildings. 'They are coming down like ninepins,' he told me at the time. 'It is short-sighted and mad in a county that relies so much on its tourism.

'We are losing far too many old buildings. There needs to be much more public interest.' Since then the interest has grown, with organised groups, and the old houses and castles such as Pengersick have been recognised as invaluable and irreplaceable gems.

The Castle is not open to the general public, but organised groups and people with a particular interest, can arrange visits on application.

One of the most successful men around our shore in this century was Sir Edward Bolitho. Lord Lieutenant, and Chairman of the Cornwall County Council, he was a dominant figure in public life and in his banking career, with the imagination to leave his family and the local people a legacy of beauty in the gardens of his home, Trengwainton.

Protected by the local climate, by the surrounding woodlands and by human care, many tender plants are grown. Trees and shrubs, particularly camellias and magnolias, bring gorgeous colour and perfume, and of course the banks of rhododendrons add to the scene. Sir Edward employed that famed plant collector Kingdon Ward to collect many rare plants and seeds from his expedition to South East Asia.

Some two miles from Penzance, Trengwainton was formerly the home of the Arundell family, and later of Sir Rose Price whose personality was as bright as the blooms. He improved the house and continued the work on the gardens—including the walled gardens—until his death in 1834. The Bolitho family first came there in 1867 when it was bought by Thomas Simon Bolitho.

Sir Edward, known affectionately as 'The Colonel' by all in Cornwall, was awarded the Victorian Medal of Honour for Horticulture in 1961, the same year in which he vested the property in the National Trust. The garden is open to the public, but not the house, which is the home of Major and Mrs Simon Bolitho and their family.

Boskenna Manor, near St Buryan, is also part of West Cornwall's history. The name means 'Big House on the Hill', said Mrs Betty Hill to me a few years before her death. When she lived there as a girl, the then Miss Paynter, it was a different era. The staff comprised her 'mother's maid, my maid, two housemaids, a cook and kitchenmaid, a pantryboy and butler in the house—and two ladies who came down from the village to clean'.

She met many international celebrities here, friends of her father, including Einstein. Boskenna had its own family ghosts. 'We had two,' Mrs Hill explained. 'Anne Paynter wanted to marry one of the tenants, and they got the press gang to take him away—she went down to St Loy and drowned herself. Her ghost was frequently seen in the house by many people.

'The other one was the man who walked up the back drive carrying his head under his arm, and if he saw anybody he threw it at them, and they died within the year. The old postman Campbell, who swore he saw him, came in and had to have brandy and cigars to cheer him up. He couldn't go on doing the round, and he was dead within the year.'

What a remarkable life she had. She was

A scene on the road near St Buryan, photographed for Lamorna Birch by S. J. Govier around 1902.

presented at Court to King George V and Queen Mary as a debutante, and was courted as a schoolgirl by the great Marconi. His white yacht *Elettra* was a familiar and gorgeous sight around the coast—even at Bournemouth where she was at boarding school. She was the first woman ever to speak direct to Australia over the air from his transmitter at Poldhu, and was the first to land in an aeroplane at the Isles of Scilly.

Thomas, the grocer, and post office at St Buryan, also pictured by S. J. Govier around 1902.

Above: **Celebrating the Coronation of Queen Elizabeth II in St James Street, Penzance, in 1953.**
Below: **The Queen visits Newlyn in 1980 to open the new pier.**

3

Our Golden Heritage

At the stroke of twelve noon on 8 May there is only one place to be in Cornwall. That is outside the Guildhall at Helston to watch the start of the Midday Furry Dance. The long dresses of the ladies, and the grey top hats and morning suits of the men, make a unique scene as the dancers go in and out of the houses and shops, up and down the main streets, to the familiar music of the town band.

The pattern has been unbroken down the years. The dance might well have its origin in pre-Christian times and is certainly a celebration of spring. The date is the Feast of St Michael, the town is bedecked with greenery

Left: **The mid-day dancers come through Church Street in Helston on Flora Day.** *Below*: **In 1907 the Lord Mayor of London, Sir William Treloar, receives a cheque from the Mayor, Mr John Toy, for the Cripples Fund.**

Coinagehall Street, Helston, about 1907.

and traditional flowers, and even the police-men on duty have their sprays of lily-of-the-valley.

I prefer the story that it all began as rejoicing at the passing of a plague, with the folk returning from the shelter of the woods waving flowers and branches of trees in hap-piness. Whatever the origin, make sure to get to the town early and see all the events—you will find it difficult to decide which you like the most. The costumes and revels of the Hal-an-Tow, with its special song and cere-mony, the early morning dance, the charm of the children's dance, the Midday, and later the 5 p.m. dance.

Here is one Cornish tradition that is not fading with the years. 'It is stronger today than ever,' said Mr Leslie Collins, Chairman of the Stewards. 'The desire to take part increases every year.'

The biggest problem is to meet the enor-mous enthusiasm of those wanting to dance. The numbers in the Midday are restricted to 130 couples, but altogether some 1500 dance during the day.

The Midday is the 'star' event, always a representative dance, and not confined to local people, although the principle of 'Helston Born' applies to the leading couples in all the dances. Mr Collins, who first took part in 1930—in the children's dance—told me there was a time when the main part of the Midday was organised at Trelowarren by Sir Courtenay Vyvyan, when the 'gentry' and house parties of the landed families came in their top hats and frock coats.

The tradition has not lost anything in dignity and spontaneity. The dancers are told: 'Enjoy yourselves, but let's have a little bit of decorum.' Thank goodness the stewards are determined there shall be no commer-cialisation of Flora Day. The only collection is for the hard-worked Town Band and the money needed for the big day is raised by subscription. The greenery comes from throughout the district, the primary school children gather the bluebells, and almost everyone with a garden grows the lily-of-the-valley, although it was so scarce one year that a shop had to get it from Holland.

The thousands of happy, smiling people, estimated at up to 40,000, crowd the town. 'It is one of the pleasantest things to organise because everyone is so helpful,' commented the Chairman, who has sixteen stewards, and a 'super efficient' secretary in Mr Len Oliver.

'They come back home from all over the world, and I cannot remember a year when someone has not come back to Helston especially to dance. It really is something special and we do our best to keep it that way.

It was a lovely summer afternoon when the first Gorsedd of Cornwall was held at Boscawen Un, near St Buryan, in 1928: fifty years later the golden jubilee ceremony was held at the same spot.

The Gorsedd thrives, and from that modest start with the eight Bards—initiated at Treorchy the previous month—some 750 have been honoured over the years. The Gorsedd is a force in Cornish life, the ceremony and robes are equally colourful, and its members have made great contributions to the life of the county.

I asked the present Grand Bard, Mr Hugh Miners, what those great pioneers Henry Jenner and Morton Nance would most enjoy about today's event. 'Our founding fathers would be delighted at what they saw, and particularly at the attendance, with 150–160 Bards making an impressive procession.

'They would be pleased that the language was still being used so fully, and that their dream of the Eisteddfod for Cornwall, em-

Turn back the clock and look through the telescope at Land's End from the 'First and Last' Refreshment House in England.

bracing so many of the arts, had come to fulfilment in 1983. They would be thrilled that the Gorsedd was still going strong.'

Mr Miners, 'Den Toll'—it means Revenue Man—became a Bard in 1957 at Predannack Cross, Mullion, and is the seventh Grand Bard. He believes in taking the Gorsedd to the people. 'In the 1980s and 1990s it has to have a real public face and purpose, and I would like the Gorsedd to be committed to a wide range of activity, particularly in education and culture, and in on the decision-making processes.'

Youth plays an important part, and no longer is it a gathering of senior citizens. Three or four young people become Bards each year through success in language examination, and this emphasises the view that the honour is not only for what has been done for Cornwall, but what can be done. 'We do expect them to work even harder for Cornwall, and to take inspiration and encouragement from being made a Bard. By

accepting it they accept also a moral responsibility to do this.'

The Gorsedd is today as strong as it has ever been. The offering of the Fruits of the Earth by the Lady of Cornwall, the flower dance, the Cry of Peace, and the oath of loyalty, are ceremonies that have no equal in the life of the county, and never fail to impress.

Nowadays the Land's End to John O'Groats marathon is almost commonplace. They run, walk, ride or drive, on their own, in teams or in relay, that testing nine hundred miles 'End to End'.

There is even a club for all who have covered the distance. I've had a laugh when Jimmy Savile has set off, had a lecture on diet and exercise when Dr Barbara Moore marched on, and even sat on the sofa at the hotel chatting to film star Elizabeth Taylor waiting for the arrival of that courageous youngster David Ryder.

Yes, they were there in their thousands to see Miss Taylor, but nothing will equal the national fervour and acclaim that greeted teenager Wendy Lewis, the Liverpool girl, when she set a time of 15 days, 14 hours, 32 minutes in March 1960. It won her the Butlin £1,000 first prize and today Wendy, now Mrs Faull, still lives in West Cornwall with her husband and their two sons, and keeps herself busy as farmer's wife.

'It was just a lark at first,' she recalled. 'We were all youngsters together, and my sister and I did it first—I was only sixteen then—and then within six weeks I had completed it a second time, celebrating my seventeenth birthday on the way.' In every town and village everyone would come out and cheer me on. Through Scotland there were piped

bands, and in Cornwall the spirit was marvellous.' Even today people recognise her, and ask her about it, but she never thinks about doing it again.

A year or so later with Joy, who now lives at nearby Angarrack, Wendy set off with petitions for peace, and walked to Rome where they had an audience with the Pope.

The marathon had a great boost from those 'Butlin' days. A week does not pass every summer but someone makes the final lap to Land's End…at times I believe the road from Penzance is crowded with them, thrilled at the completion of an arduous test of stamina and fitness.

I have been there to celebrate with dozens of them, but, apart from Wendy, I have two other moments captured forever. One is of the disappointment of Dr Moore that last time around, when I drove her from Penzance to Land's End the night before the start. She was clearly tired, and unwell, and after all her earlier triumphs this was a failure.

The other is of David Ryder, in August 1969, and of thousands waiting in the fog and mist to welcome this 21-year-old polio victim at the climax of his 860 mile walk on elbow crutches and in leg irons. Polio struck David when he was two years old. Although superstar Elizabeth Taylor fulfilled a promise by coming to congratulate him she was determined not to steal the show. Her remark to his mother summed it up: 'I admire your son so much.'

Tom Bawcock's Eve is more fancy than fact, but everyone enjoys the fun. Go to Mousehole on the night before Christmas Eve, and you will hear them singing the cheerful tune at the Ship Inn and at the Coastguard Hotel.

A merry place you may believe
Was Mousehole 'pon Tom Bawcock's Eve.
is the start of the song, and its chorus. The tale of the starving village, and the huge catch of seven sorts of fish to feed the people at Christmas, is delightful and is nowadays 'enshrined' in the fish pie with the heads sticking up out of the crust.

Above: **Mr Nicholas Matthews, who farms at Gulval, holds aloft the 'neck'.** *Right*: **The Sunday School banner is held high in 1908 during the St Peterstide celebrations.**

This, though, is a 'modern tradition' which goes down well with the visitors, is encouraged by the locals, and is good for the beer-drinking business. There is no record of Tom Bawcock being a member of the Band of Hope in his day, but he must have been a great fisherman.

Starry-Gazey Pie is now in the recipe books for all the 'foreigners' who come to Cornwall seeking new dishes.

May Day seems to have lost so much of its original character. Although it is now a public holiday and more of a Labour Day with 'Red Flag' overtones, many will remember those less sophisticated years. Then the parents would prepare the May whistles, the 'Feepers', after cutting the twigs and trimming the

44

bark, and we children would revel in playing these, blowing our Mayhorns and marching with our pointed colourful hats. It was a Children's Day, full of innocence and celebration.

Still flourishing, down the centuries, is the 'Crying the Neck' ceremony, now stronger than ever. Although the Old Cornwall Societies have been responsible for reviving the harvest custom, it is one that any group can organise, and particularly relevant for Young Farmers' Clubs.

'The Neck' is the last few heads of corn, waved aloft in the field by the farmer to announce that the last of the harvest has been cut and to symbolise that the 'corn spirit' has been caught. This neck is taken into the farmhouse and kept there for the next year to ensure another good harvest. Always popular, with its Cornish dialect and language, it is now often ended with a church harvest festival service to give it a good Christian emphasis.

From Chapel Carn Brea near Land's End to Helston and the Lizard and on to Kit Hill near the Cornish border, the Cornish get 'lit up' every 23 June, Midsummer Eve. From twelve to twenty bonfires carry the evening message from hill to hill. Again it is a pagan ceremony in origin, for it was a great day for the sun-worshipping people who preceded the Celts here, and also a fertility ceremony.

'It has never really died,' Grand Bard Mr Hugh Miners told me, 'but now it has a new shape and purpose, and personality. We burn 48 separate and specific herbs and wild flowers in the sheaf which is thrown on the fire by the Lady of the Flowers. She does this so that the flames will burn the weeds, destroying evil and strengthening good. I can remember in the old days, when the fire had burned down, that we youngsters would dance around it, singing songs, and leap over it.'

It is an invigorating night, full of ancient mysteries...and hot pasties.

The Sunday School banners are still carried, and the large saffron buns eaten for the St Peterstide Celebrations at Porthleven.

St Peter, the Patron Saint of Fishermen, has a special place in the affection of the people here. At one time the chapels had their parades on separate days, but then the Fore Street and Peverell Road Methodist churches joined for this event, and just a few years back invited the Church of England to be with them.

Now there is an ecumenical united Procession of Witness on the nearest Saturday to 29 June. There is a parade around the harbour and the village, with the two large banners, and with two bands. A wreath is laid at the war memorial and there is tea at the recreation ground: what a day for the youngsters!

Mr Bert Cowls, who joined in this parade around 1910 when he was a young lad, remembered the special gingerbread they enjoyed, made by Mr Charlie Cowls at his Porthleven bakery. 'So carefully was the secret kept that when he died the recipe was lost.'

The custom of giving an 'Allan Apple', a great monster of an apple, was very popular in the Penzance and Newlyn district. 'You slept with it under your pillow so you could dream of your sweetheart,' popular singer Brenda Wootton told me. The tradition seems to have died out, but I hope Brenda's singing of Richard Gendall's song, that tells the story, helps to revive the delightful custom, at Hallowe'en.

Right: **The Trustees of the Ebenezer Primitive Methodist Church at Newlyn in November 1927, pictured outside the chapel in Boase Street. From left to right, standing: Messrs James White, William Henry Williams, William Roberts, John White, Joe P. Harvey. Front row: Messrs William Reynolds, James Treneer, Rev. R. F. Wearmouth, Philip White, Charles Jenkin, James Mann Johns.**

The Marazion Wesleyan tea treat on Treglown's
picnic grounds in 1910.

4

The Rescue Heroes

'They were truly the bravest eight men I have ever seen.' Those words by Lt Cdr Russell L. Smith, of the US navy, pilot of a Sea King helicopter that flew from RNAS Culdrose over the stricken coaster *Union Star*, best sum up the emotions of all when the tragedy of the Penlee lifeboat *Solomon Browne* is remembered.

The events of that Saturday night of 19 December in 1981 have left an indelible mark not only at Mousehole, and in Cornwall, but in the annals of the RNLI and in the hearts of people worldwide. All eight lifeboatmen died in trying to save those on the coaster in hurricane force winds and huge seas at Tater-Du, near Lamorna Cove.

To Coxswain Trevelyan Richards went the Gold Medal of the RNLI—the lifeboatman's VC—and the Bronze Medal went to all the members of the crew, Stephen Madron, Nigel Brockman, Charles Greenhaugh, John Blewett, Kevin Smith, Barrie Torrie, and Gary Wallis. All eight on board the *Union Star* also died, including the Master, his wife and her two daughters.

This Penlee story, and the memory of the coaster impaled on the rocks, sums up the theme of rescue and wreck around Mount's Bay, and the courage of those who take the rough waves with the smooth. They gave their lives in order to save their fellows, even when they were strangers.

As one who recorded the tragedy, day by day for several months, many images remain in clear focus: the traumatic and chilling knowledge, when the fragments of the lifeboat came floating in, that all was lost; the silence through Mousehole that grim Sunday; the aching grief that poured out on Christmas Eve at the funeral service at Paul Church; the response by the men who immediately volunteered to crew a new lifeboat; the dignity of the families who mourned.

Their loss, so close to Christmas, had an electric effect, and millions of pounds poured into the appeal fund so admirably handled by the Penwith Council. I recall the visit of the Duke and Duchess of Kent for the Remembrance Service, and the gifts of a silver cross to each widow or mother, and later the dedication of the unique granite and crystal memorial at the church, the nine-hour inquest and very lengthy public inquiry at Penzance.

Within days of the tragedy the money for a new boat had been given, and on a summer's day in 1983 I watched a new chapter in Penlee history begin with the naming of the *Mabel Alice* in Newlyn Harbour. This came just a couple of days after twenty had died when the Sikorsky helicopter from Penzance crashed into the sea near the Isles of Scilly.

Mr John Corin of the Penlee branch, and co-author of its lifeboat history, agreed with me that the naming ceremony of the *Mabel*

Alice by the Duke of Kent was the start of a new chapter. 'While those who have gone will never be forgotten, life compels us to look ahead,' he added.

All the crew of twenty on the roll are fully trained with Ken Thomas continuing the tradition of Coxswain as a successful fisherman. Already the new boat has been to the rescue many times, and shown her paces in the bay.

'The modern man has to be more of a technician as well as have high qualities of seamanship, and achieve a high standard in medical examination. The standard of formal training now is very high, while in the old days anyone who went to sea was automatically qualified.

The splendid new Penlee lifeboat, *Mabel Alice*, named by the Duke of Kent, in 1983. She is a 52-foot Arun-class lifeboat, with a speed of 18 knots.

'He had to pull an oar and the Coxswain could see the wreck, and knew where it was, and navigated by eye. The modern boat is crammed with radar and Decca, a direction finder and echo sounders, to operate over a greater range and in thicker weather. The standard of specialised seamanship and boat-handling on the part of the Coxswain and Second Coxswain is very high indeed.'

Mr Corin, who counts the loss of HMS *Anson* as the worst wreck in Mount's Bay— way back on 29 December in 1807—told me that as well as the sophisticated technology of modern lifeboats, there are only half the number of men on board compared with the old days.

When the mainmast of the 44-gun frigate *Anson* fell, it made a bridge for many on board to escape to Loe Bar beach. But over 120 drowned including Captain Charles Lydiard who was lost in trying to save a young lad.

Over the years many dives have taken place on the wreck, and in April 1905 a large cannon was raised, first of several down the years, including a 32-pounder iron cannon, three and a half tons in weight, which stands outside the Helston Museum.

'It was a day I shall never forget,' said Mr Johnny Drew, mechanic for thirty-five years of the Penlee lifeboat. The day was Wednesday 23 April in 1947—and those who saw the rescue from HMS *Warspite* aground on the Cudden Ledges near Prussia Cove, will have it also imprinted on their memories.

Here was one of the great British battleships, on her way to the scrapheap, featuring in one of the most dramatic incidents in

lifeboat history in Cornwall. Eight men—the skeleton crew—on this 30,000 ton giant were lifted off.

None told it better to me than Mr Drew who was associated with the lifeboat for forty-seven years, during which time 171 lives were saved from shipwreck. Mr Eddie Madron, skipper of the fishing boat *Renovelle* was making his first trip as the new Coxswain, and he received the Silver Medal of the RNLI for his skills and Mr Drew the Bronze for his 'very efficient handling' of the engines.

'On going down across the bay the *Warspite* was already out of sight from us,' the mechanic commented. 'She had been driven in close to Cudden so the lifeboat continued until they were right ahead of the battleship.

'With good seamanship the Coxswain decided that he would turn and run in towards the *Warspite*. This we did and it was a terrific sea. Two or three seas swept the lifeboat, but

A proud moment at Porthleven as a cannon from the *Anson* is salvaged in 1905.

The maroons sounded on Sunday when the *Yewcroft*, an 827-ton steamer, went aground in fog in July 1956. She broke her back within a few hours to bring a swift end at Trevean, Cudden Point, to this voyage from the Thames around to Bristol. The crew's navigation was so astray that they thought they were near the Brisons. All were saved by the Penlee lifeboat except for the Chief Engineer who was rescued by rocket line fired by the LSA crew.

all was well, and we reduced speed and the Coxswain saw a channel about forty yards wide on the port side of the *Warspite*. We took the lifeboat into this, got in under her port quarter, manoeuvred the lifeboat around in a very small space, and endeavoured to bring her up to the port side of the *Warspite*.'

Mr Drew and the second engineer were on their knees under the canopy: they couldn't stand because of the huge seas.

As the heavy sea was coming towards the lifeboat, the Coxswain would call 'Full Ahead' on the engines to keep the lifeboat in position against the sea. Then 'Full Astern' to keep it in position from the turmoil of the surf from the cliffs behind us.

'We had a rise and fall of thirty foot. On top of that sea we would be up and level with the *Warspite's* deck. Then a crew member would jump—and we would be down again

The Penlee lifeboat, with Coxswain Eddie Madron and crew, comes alongside the stricken HMS *Warspite* off Cudden Point in April 1947.

It is from the fishermen that lifeboat crews are mainly drawn. Here is a sturdy crew aboard their lugger at Newlyn about 1900. Left to right, back row: Edgar Reynolds, William Harvey, — —, William Simons. Front: Willie Harvey, Willie Bone.

in a few seconds. This went on for thirty-five minutes, up and down, until we had taken the eight crew members on board.'

The *Warspite* was moved a short distance later, but ended her days on the beach off Marazion, slowly reduced to scrap metal.

'There is no more extraordinary stretch in Britain than at the end of the southern peninsula, where the Lizard plunges towards the sea. The cliffs are fierce; rocks and reefs make a deadly cincture about them. Every jut, every cove, could tell some tale of storm. On a winter night, with the sea in the "white-lipped wrath", the Lizard can terrify.' So wrote Mr J. C. Trewin, that great talent who went 'up from the Lizard' to make a splendid literary reputation.

How true his remarks are, as those remarkable men who have been Coxswain of the local lifeboat over the years testify, famous names such as Matthews and Mitchell, Roberts and Rowe, Stephens and Legge…and today another Mitchell is the Coxswain. Mr Peter Mitchell, now in his fifties, must be one of the most experienced lifeboatmen in the South West, for he has been Coxswain—

Mechanic of the Lizard–Cadgwith boat since 1976, mechanic since 1957, and a member of the crew from 1952.

In the ninety two years up to 1952, more than forty vessels, ranging from ketches to ocean liners had been wrecked or in peril, on the short length of coast between Kynance Cove and the Lizard Church Cove, and from them the Lizard lifeboats had saved 601 lives.

There was tragedy with the first lifeboat at the Lizard, the *Anne Maria* rowing six oars. While on exercise in January 1866 she capsized in a hurricane and the Coxswain, again a Mr Peter Mitchell, and two of the crew, Mr Richard Harris and Mr Nicholas Stevens were drowned. A new boat was provided and the same name retained, with the lifeboat house near Polpeor beach.

Curiously enough it was way back in 1907 that the last RNLI medal was awarded here, and the only awards in recent years have been a certificate marking the Fastnet Race rescue and letters of commendation for the part played after the loss of the *Solomon Browne*

Black Head close to the Lizard is well named. Many ships have been lost here including the *Gunvor* in April 1912. She was so close to shore that a bowsprit overhung the rocks and the crew got to safety by rope ladder.

of Penlee in 1981, and in 1962 when the *Ardgarry* capsized off the Lizard.

Not a trace of the *Ardgarry* was found, nor a member of the crew, but the present Coxswain will never forget that night at sea after a flare was sighted three miles to the south west. 'We have never launched before in such conditions,' he told me at his home at Parc Grous.

'The wind was gusting from the east at 90 to 100 miles, and blowing 60 m.p.h. all day into our station. We had a call in darkness in December, just before Christmas, and the sea had built up so much that it came up the slipway, knocked in the front of the doors and was sweeping up through the boathouse.

Coxswain Peter Mitchell of the Lizard-Cadgwith lifeboat.

'When we launched in this storm the boat stood up on end, thrown up so high that we thought it would go bow over stern. That night our radio aerials were blown down and we lost contact with the land. They were very worried on shore that we might have been lost.'

Coxswain Mitchell knew the crew of Penlee well, and recalled that when they went to search at midnight that December 1981 the conditions were even worse. 'We didn't realise until the next day that the four-inch bilge keels had split on our boat, the *Duke of Cornwall*, and she was half-full of water. The pressure of the water as we dropped down off the big seas had done this. It was a frightening night: we had to round the Lizard and the boat was crashing on the seas as though it was hitting rock.'

The Lizard lifeboat, *Admiral Sir George Back*, on service from 1903-18. She was built at a cost of £780 at Blackheath, with a legacy from Mrs Eliza Back.

The present Lizard-Cadgwith station at Kilcobben Cove was opened in 1961. It brought the two together, with Cadgwith closing a couple of years later.

The old Lizard crew took over the new boat, but there were several Cadgwith men aboard, such as George Mitchell and Mr Bunny Legge, even though they have over three miles to travel compared with the Lizard men's half a mile. Today there is also a Mullion man in the crew: he travels five miles, and makes almost every call.

Most of the crew were not even born when Coxswain Mitchell first joined—he started his thirty-third year with the lifeboat in February 1984. They get an average of eight to ten calls a year, and cover from Porthleven

in the west to Coverack and the dreaded Manacles. 'It is a terrible coastline from Lizard Head down to Gunwalloe, and very remote,' he commented.

'What makes the Lizard so bad is that we have a tide race of three to four knots off the headland which makes a confused sea when wind is against tide...and even on the ebb when there is no wind. You can see the big waves turning, like an overfall, to make a broken sea.'

There have been many great moments in the lifeboat's history. Coxswain William Edward Mitchell and Second Coxswain Edwin Mitchell were awarded the silver medal of the RNLI in 1907 in going to the rescue of the 456 passengers and crew of the White Star Liner *Suevic*, wrecked in fog on the Clidgas Rocks at Polpeor. All were saved by the Lizard, Cadgwith, Coverack and Porthleven lifeboats, with the Lizard's ten-oared thirty-five foot self-righting boat *Admiral Sir George Back* bringing off 167.

55

Turn the clock forward to 29 July 1935 when the twin-engined motor lifeboat went to the rescue after the big tanker *D. L. Harper* ran on to the Crane Ledges near Caerthillian Cove. The crew of forty three were taken off after standing by the ship in the fog all night.

Everyone can still remember the heroism of Captain Carlsen and Mr Dancey who stayed on board the *Flying Enterprise* after the tug *Turmoil*'s tow rope parted and it looked as though the listing steamship would sink in the gale. The Lizard boat cruised around her at close quarters for four hours as *Flying Enterprise* lay at an angle of almost seventy degrees.

The present Coxswain has vivid memories of recent rescues. In June 1979 the fifteen men on the 2,000 tonne coaster *Shoreham*, on her way from North Wales to Belgium with limestone, were saved and ended up having breakfast in Mrs Thelma Mitchell's kitchen. The vessel went ashore on the Lizard side of Mullion Island, and all came off on the *Duke of Cornwall* except the skipper, who was very reluctant to leave and had to be persuaded by the coastguards later. One member had a prayer mat under his arm and wouldn't eat the fried bacon. Later the ship was towed off and taken to Falmouth.

Many yachts have been towed after getting in trouble with September gales: in 1983 the lifeboat brought one twenty-six miles in a north east gale to Newlyn with three people aboard.

Culdrose cannot help but make headlines. This Royal Naval Air Station is as vital to Helston's economy as it is to our defence

The crew of the coaster *Shoreham* are landed by the Lizard-Cadgwith lifeboat.

Old and new over Mount's Bay: with the fixed-wing Airborne Early Warning Gannet—the last flying in this country—is the AEW Sea King helicopter of 824 Squadron.

system and the local twenty-four-hour rescue service.

Millions of pounds come into circulation from the pay packets, for there are about 6,000 service personnel and their dependants in the area. There is a monthly pay bill of £1.5 million.

It is frightening to contemplate the effect on the town if *Seahawk* should close, yet it was just over thirty-five years ago that it was commissioned as the Naval Air Fighter School. From 750 acres of farmland has come the largest naval air station in the country and the biggest helicopter base in Europe.

Prince Andrew is a famous 'old boy' of Culdrose, based here for three years. He did his training, received his wings from his father, Prince Philip, in 1981, and during the Falklands campaign helped protect HMS *Invincible* and other ships of the Task Force.

Although one remembers the dramatic rescues by the men of 771 Squadron, particularly of seventy four survivors from the Fastnet Race tragedy in 1979, the main task is the support of the Front Line Squadrons flying the Sea King Mark Five anti-submarine warfare helicopters.

The primary role is to hunt and kill submarines, and in the Falklands War Culdrose provided this capability with over 1,000 men down South at the height of the conflict.

When there has been a crisis at sea or on shore around Mount's Bay in recent years, a Culdrose team has almost always been there to rescue the victims. Whether it be the lifting of survivors from the *Jeanne Goughy* at Land's End in 1962, or the efforts to find possible survivors from the British Airways helicopter tragedy off the Isles of Scilly in 1983, a Culdrose crew has been at work. Hundreds must have been saved over the years and it has not only been people who have been lifted clear. In May 1980 twelve cows were brought to the safety of the clifftop near Portholland after stampeding.

A public viewing enclosure, car park and picnic area are open at Culdrose throughout the year. The Fleet Air Arm Museum shop is open in spring and summer.

Lifeboats and helicopters can be sure of banner headlines, but in West Cornwall the controlling role of the coastguard service is a crucial one.

The past few years have seen a fresh command structure, with Prince Charles, Honorary Commodore, opening the new Coastguard Maritime Rescue Co-ordination Centre at Falmouth in December 1981.

It was the first in the world to be directly linked to a coast earth station at Goonhilly. New technology has overtaken so many of the old methods: a sophisticated network now keeps contact with the ship in trouble and with the rescue services—from police to pilots, from lifeboats to Royal Navy, from ambulances to auxiliaries, whether at sea, on shore or in the sky.

There are six regions in the country, and at Falmouth the Regional Controller is Captain Peter Harris, who took over in April 1982. The morning I spoke to him, there had been an alert: a 35,000 tonne bulk carrier, with twenty-eight people on board, asking for a vessel to stand by her in the south west gales raging at Force 9 some ninety-five miles west of the Bishop Rock Lighthouse.

'We have an enormous range of activity from sail-boards to bulk carrier ships and oil drilling, and hundreds of thousands of pleasure craft. Not only do we have this great range, but more of it than anywhere else,' Captain Harris remarked. There are six regions in the country and at Falmouth the control is over thousands of squares miles of sea. The local district is from Dodman Point in the south to Tintagel Head on the north coast, while the search and rescue region stretches from Selsey Bill out into mid-Atlantic up to the west coast of Ireland, and to the north of the Spanish coast.

There is still a role for the man with local knowledge, for although there are one hundred regular coastguards in the region there are 1,800 auxiliaries. Casualty risk watch stations are maintained around Mount's Bay at the Lizard, Mullion, Porthleven, Penzer Point, and at Gwennap Head near Land's End. The part-time coastguards have their look-out and cliff-rescue sections, with their sector officers, Don Buckfield at Penzance and Land's End, and Bill Hogg at Lizard and Porthleven, training and organising.

No one should underestimate the contribution made by Land's End Radio, now based at Skewjack, near Sennen. The staff here are often the 'forgotten men', as far as the general public is concerned, but they play a vital part in ship-to-shore communication and are almost always the first with news of a potential crisis at sea. A campaign has begun to ensure that it remains a manned station, despite financial economies, and this must succeed.

It was almost Easter, the weather was improving, and those dependent on the 1967 holiday season were waiting for the 'off'. The date was Saturday 18 March and, when the news first came through to me at the newspaper office of the grounding of a ship called the *Torrey Canyon* on the Seven Stones reef, there was no way of realising its significance.

These were among the most dramatic days in West Cornwall history. It was the news story Cornwall didn't expect and didn't want, and those who saw the oil reach the beaches at Sennen and the harbour at Porthleven will never forget the black carpet. The stench from the pollution swept over the county: I could smell it at Truro one afternoon. This tanker was over twice the length of a football pitch, 974 feet and carried 119,000 tons of crude oil on board. By Sunday lunchtime the slick was twelve miles long, and the next day had stretched to twenty-two miles. Slowly it was realised what this could mean to the local economy. The detergent and the experts came pouring in. A Dutch salvage chief was killed in an engine room explosion.

Captain Jim Summerlee was the first man to see the *Torrey Canyon* on the rocks while on his helicopter trip from Penzance to St Mary's. 'We first smelt it,' he told me. 'We were six to seven miles downwind of it, and the smell of the oil throughout the aircraft was such that it worried me about her safety.' He asked for the instruments to be checked for fear of an oil leak. Then he looked around and saw the tanker with oil coming out, and at first thought it was being done intentionally to possibly launch a boat.

'I called air traffic control at St Mary's and told them I thought the tanker was aground,

The Belgian trawler *Victoire Roger* wrecked at Tallis Zawn, Land's End, in March 1964. Trinity House had just announced that a light and fog signal was being placed at Tater Du. All on board were saved by the brilliant work of the coxswain and crew of the Sennen Cove lifeboat.

RN helicopters alongside the giant tanker *Torrey Canyon* at Easter 1967 when she went aground on the Sevenstones Reef.

and as far as I knew that was the first record,' he added.

Captain Summerlee, then aged forty three, saw the wreck more than anyone over the next few weeks, for his passengers all wanted to be taken that way. Every trace finally went from the scene. 'It hardly seems possible that a ship of that size should disappear so entirely.'

When he looked back, years later, he remarked: 'It was ironic that it should happen so close to the Isles of Scilly, and like the Fortunate Islands they are, it only reached the eastern isles, but never actually polluted them. But it certainly came to almost my doorstep at Sennen, thick and muddy all over the beach.'

He called it 'a most horrifying sight and most terrible memory'. There were no white waves, no golden sands, no life at all. 'It changed the whole texture of the sand and made it into quicksand, thousands of oiled birds being washed up. I can recall some people crying, literally, and saying 'You will never see Sennen clean again.'

There were fears of permanent damage, but Nature has cleared all that and Sennen has long been back to normal. The whole disaster, however, awakened the world to the need for vigilance, and brought two words and a new name to the language of the environment— *Torrey Canyon*.

The wreck of the *Torrey Canyon* wrote a horrific chapter in the world-wide history of oil pollution. At Porthleven harbour (*right*) efforts are being made to clean up the oil.

5

Those Magnificent Ladies

It is over a century since a wife was last offered for sale in Cornwall—she went for sixpence at the market—and things have changed so dramatically that I am waiting for the first report of a husband being put up for auction!

We might even live to see the day when there is a woman chairman of Cornwall County Council. What hope of a Lady Bishop of Truro in the twenty-first century?

Women in our district have for years been proving what they can do in the community. They have made invaluable contributions, and many of those who have given outstanding service have come to live among us.

One of my favourite ladies of Mount's Bay is Miss Dorothy Yglesias, who died in her ninetieth year in February 1980 just a short while before she was due to receive a much-deserved MBE at Buckingham Palace. She truly became a legend in her own lifetime with her work for the Mousehole bird hospital and sanctuary which she founded with her sister 'Pog' over a half-century before.

She gave all her time, effort and money to the cause, and even when the RSPCA said they could not continue supporting it financially, again took on the work and continued until her death. She always spoke so well, and with so much honesty and sincerity, that it was a joy to meet and talk with her.

It was in 1912 that she first came to Mousehole, and stayed in lodgings on holiday. 'We lost our hearts to it at once. When we saw this hill the first night, we said "That will be our favourite walk". We little thought one day we would be living here.' But in 1925 the sisters persuaded mother to sell the London house after father died, and settle in Mousehole. They had never specialised in anything to do with birds. They never had the money, only the desire, to do things, and bought the 'wonderful stretch' of land where they built their homes and hospital.

Jacko was the first bird to be cared for by them—the bird turned out to be a Jacqueline—but tame and fearless Jimmy the Crow became an institution at Mousehole, 'top dog' one might say, for over twenty years after being found in a nest with dead birds around him, near Helston.

Her story of the young boy who brought a jackdaw with a broken wing seems to sum up her qualities. 'I held out my hands to take the bird,' she told me, 'and he drew back. I said "Oh let me look" and he said "you do grow new wings here, don't you?" I replied "We do our very utmost, and I promise you faithfully that if we can't grow a new wing, which I think we may not be able to do, it is so bad, we shall give him a friend to live with and we shall make him happy as long as he lives."

'And that child's face, I shall never forget

it. It relaxed with the sweetest smile and he gave me the bird with the utmost trust, and I felt that child had been through an experience that would leave its mark in some way.'

Year after year the birds returned to see the sisters, some wanting to come into the little studio to sleep again where they were reared. Dorothy and Pog never thought they would carry on for so many years, nor that the hospital would achieve such a world-wide reputation. Their age was no barrier to their selfless dedication, and when the shock came that they again had to take over in 1975, gifts came from around the world, including such contributors as the Aga Khan and Prince Bernhardt.

The staff stood by them. 'It has been an absolute triumph,' Dorothy said later. With such leaders as Mr Bill Young the dream came true at the bird hospital for the second time in her life. Imagine the scope of the local tragedies when it is realised that over one thousand birds come here each year.

I have always felt that there is a distinct Cornish atmosphere about the novels of the Brontë sisters. Yorkshire may have been their home, and Howarth the Brontë shrine, but the power, mystery and sense of foreboding apparent in such classics as *Wuthering Heights* and *Jane Eyre* seem as Cornish as Lanyon Quoit and Tregoning Hill, with sou'west winds and driving rain.

The late Dorothy Yglesias MBE, co-founder of the Mousehole Wild Bird Hospital and Sanctuary, feeding some of the patients.

Fishermen check their boats at Mousehole.

So it comes as little surprise to learn that their maternal grandparents were born and bred, and lived in busy Chapel Street at Penzance, that was a main thoroughfare to the harbour front in those days 160 years ago. It was also a principal residential area for those prominent in the business life of the district.

'Mr Thomas Branwell was such a man, a merchant and property owner, and a councillor of the Corporation,'said Miss Frances Branwell. She is the only person now bearing the Branwell name in the town, and was looking forward to her eighty-fifth birthday in May 1984 when she spoke to me.

'He lived with his wife Ann at number 25, but both died in 1808. Four years later Maria, then 29, made the journey to visit an uncle and aunt at Woodhouse Grove School, a Methodist boys' school in Yorkshire. She never saw Cornwall again for she married the Reverend Patrick Brontë on 29 December, and died at Haworth some eight years later.'

Miss Branwell, a first cousin four times removed from Maria, told me: 'In those eight years she had six children, three of whom, Emily, Anne and Charlotte, became the most famous sisters in English literature. Aunt Elizabeth, Maria's sister, went to Yorkshire and for over twenty years took charge of the family. The Brontë girls did not visit Cornwall, but the influence of Elizabeth, her Cornish sense, her devotion and love of the girls must have been immeasurable. She also helped finance Charlotte and Emily's education in Brussels.

'On the same day as Maria married in Yorkshire her cousin Jane Fennell was married in the same church, and at Penzance her sister Charlotte married her cousin Joseph Branwell at Madron.

'Maria as a girl looks like Miss Julia Tripp, my great-niece, so the family resemblance is there almost two hundred years on. And I have built up a full family tree back to 1657 when John Branwell married,' said Miss Branwell.

A plaque outside the house in Chapel Street was unveiled in September 1975 during the Mayoralty of Mr Jim Batten, and in 1983 the Brontë Society marked the bi-centenary of Maria's birth with a visit to Penzance. The members were thrilled to see the home so lovingly cared for, following its restoration by Miss Lilian Oldham, who still lives there, and Miss Sylvia Richards, who died a few years ago.

There is no theatre in Britain with the special qualities of the Minack, tucked away along those Porthcurno rocks. Approach it from the air, come across it at sea as you round a headland, or suddenly enter it from the cliffside, and it is equally astonishing.

There is always an element of surprise here because the theatre is part of nature as well as in conflict with it. Would you get planning permission for it today? Just over fifty years ago that stage and auditorium were at the bottom of the gully next to a cliff garden. The

The corner of Wood Street at Penzance and a cottage destroyed by fire in the 1890s. It was in 1812 that Maria Branwell left Penzance for Yorkshire.

The first post-war production at the Minack Theatre, *The Trojan Women*, was directed by Miss G. M. Tranter with pupils from both Penzance Girls' and Boys' Grammar Schools. The author is second from left. The *Yeomen of the Guard* are on duty (*left*) during the production by St Just Operatic Society.

granite outcrops became the wings, the rows of seats were cut and shaped, the theatre created.

It is to a woman, Miss Rowena Cade, the Minack owes its being. Her home became her destiny, her garden a magnet for thousands of visitors each summer as they watch Shakespeare or Shaw—in drama or in musical—Ibsen or A. A. Milne, Gilbert and Sullivan, or Dylan Thomas, who lived at one time a mile up the road.

The inspiration came from a production of *A Midsummer Night's Dream* nearby, which led to *The Tempest* at the Minack House cliff garden, both with music by Penzance Orchestral Society. Mr J. Morgan Hosking, for so many years its conductor, still recalls those happy events.

Day by day, year by year, the work went on, with the theatre developing from that first amateur show in August 1932. Mainly with the aid of Billy Rawlings, hundreds of tons of rock and earth were moved, a staggering task in more ways than one.

I had the joy of taking part in the first production after the war years, in 1949, and again in 1954, as the theatre steadily re-established itself. Then it was in the tragedies by Euripides that we trod the green turf stagecloth, with little thought of midnight matinées. When I was there again in recent years in *Merrie England* for the Queen's Silver Jubilee, and in the Gilbert and Sullivan opera *Yeoman of the Guard* it was a different scene.

Big changes indeed: much more concrete, many more sophisticated theatrical facilities for players and for audiences. Yet the magic remains, on a moonlit night or, as I prefer, a sunbathed summer afternoon, the matchless background of Mount's Bay, Lizard Light and Logan Rock still undiminished. I shall always remember Miss Cade perched high on the rocks above her theatre, absorbed in the entertainment below.

Mrs Dora Russell, ninety in April 1984, is one of England's most remarkable women. She walked with Lenin, talked with Shaw, and for twelve years was married to the philosopher Bertrand Russell.

It was in 1922 that the decision came to live in Cornwall, and she still has her home there at that first choice, Carn Voel, Porthcurno. Still as strong as ever is her progressive philosophy towards women, and she continues to write and to campaign, as she has done throughout her public life, which has taken her to China, the United States, India and Russia and other major countries of the world.

Mrs Dora Russell of Porthcurno.

It is good to know that there is now a plaque in Mousehole to mark the home of Dolly Pentreath, but for years there has been a monument to her in the wall of the churchyard at Paul where she was buried in 1777. This was put here in June 1860 by Prince Louis Luçien Bonaparte for Dolly, 'said to have been the last person who conversed in the ancient Cornish, the peculiar language of this county from the earliest records till it expired in the eighteenth century in this parish of Saint Paul'.

The Grand Bard, Hugh Miners believes beyond doubt that she would understand the Cornish language we speak today. 'The only sad thing is that so much died with her—we would have understood a great deal more if what she said had been recorded.

'She was quite a character, and so has grown up the myth that she was the last native speaker of the language, and she was certainly almost the last. And it is interesting that from the ceremonies in 1877 to mark the centenary of her death came the increasing interest in Cornish-ness and the language.'

A fine painting of Dolly, by John Opie, hangs at St Michael's Mount.

Mary Kelynack's cottage at the Fradgan is no more. Up until recent years a little wooden plaque announced that from this Newlyn home she 'walked to London in 1851 and met Queen Victoria'. It was the year of the Great Exhibition, and Mary, aged 84, trudged the three hundred miles or more to visit the Crystal Palace. She caught the attention of *The Times*, *The Illustrated London News* artist pictured her, and after her days as a celebrity she made a triumphant progress back home.

The Queen herself recorded: 'The old Cornish woman, who walked up several hundred miles to see the Exhibition was at the door to see me—a most hale old woman who was near crying at my looking at her.'

Some of the nicest moments came at the Mansion House where Mary was received by the Lady Mayoress, had a long chat and a cup of tea, but did even better with the Lord

Mayor. She told him she had come from the Land's End to attend to a 'little matter as well as see the Exhibition', and told him that she only had fivepence halfpenny.

A report of the occasion added: 'After a little conversation which caused merriment, the Lord Mayor made her a present of a sovereign. On receiving the gift the old woman burst into tears, and said: "Now I shall be able to get back."'

What stories this old fishwife must have had to tell. She had made her living carrying fish from Penzance for sale in the traditional 'cowal', and had probably been no further than Camborne before her 'sponsored walk'. It is thought she may have gone to enquire if her late husband's pension continued after his death—he was a retired naval man—and there are rumours that she was much younger than the eighty-four years claimed.

It was from Newlyn (*above*) that Mary Kelynack set out for London. She was a fishseller at Penzance. At a later date (*left*) Dick Renfree and Alma Hosking ply their trade at Victoria Terrace near the bottom of Morrab Road.

6

Those Saints kept Marching In

There is more than enough history, tradition and legend to enjoy at the Churches of the Saints around Mount's Bay to complete a fortnight's holiday. From St Buriena to St Winwaloe the names ring out.

The churches tell the history down the centuries better than any other record and hold an astonishing richness of variety in their treasures. Architecture and local history, music and drama, war and peace, art and craftsmanship: all have a place here. Let me tell you a few of their stories...then make a point of going to see for yourselves. My visits in 1984 confirmed that in every case the

Cornish church door remains open for the visitor and the worshipper.

Can anyone have been a Cornish vicar longer than Reverend William Wriothesley Wingfield, of **Gulval,** from 30 May in 1839 until his death on 16 November in 1912, a total of seventy-three years? What a record. The clock and two treble bells marked his fiftieth anniversary in 1889.

Of special interest in this most charming of buildings—and most popular for weddings— is a fourteenth-century font with its carvings. Part of the shaft of a Saxon cross found in the 1860s is outside the church porch, while on the desk by the door is the Lord's Prayer in Cornish, reminding worshippers of the antiquity of the Christian faith in the county.

An unusual ceremony is linked with the

splendidly ornate monument to William Bolitho, of Ponsandane who died in 1894. He left interest on money to be given on the anniversary of his death to five deserving widows or spinsters of seventy or over. He asked it to be given at his graveside on each 2 December, but it is now given beside his memorial…no doubt because of bad winter weather in the cemetery.

At **St Buryan** the long rood screen has a curious hunting story to tell of dragon and fish, donkey and stag—even a lobster. It is believed to be symbolic of the warfare between good and evil.

In the graveyard lies one of the greatest men to leave their mark during the past two centuries on Westcountry history, Augustus Smith, for thirty-eight years 'Lord Proprietor of the Isles of Scilly'. He laid the foundation of their present prosperity, and died at Plymouth in July 1872 aged sixty eight.

Tradition has it that King Athelstan rested in the cell attached to the small Oratory of St Buryan the night before he sailed to conquer the Isles of Scilly. He vowed that if successful he would found and endow a church.

Don't leave without finding the splendid Celtic crosses. One is in the churchyard, just outside the main south porch, and believed to be eighth-century. One side shows the crucifixion and the other the five hemispheres, symbolising the five wounds of our Lord. In the road, outside the front gate is an eleventh-century market cross.

The charming little **St Levan** Church, tucked away beyond Porthcurno and the Minack, is largely fifteenth-century, but its font with a star and cable mouldings is from

Left: **The Jester on the bench-end at St Levan Church.** *Far left*: **Canon Charles Buckley, Vicar of Gulval, blesses the mead. The Mayor of St Ives, Alderman John Payne, is on his right and on his left are Penzance Aldermen Jim Trezise, Horace Jackson and Gordon Rowe.**

the twelfth, and could be from an earlier church here. The bench-ends are full of interest and humour. There is the pilgrim with his beard, hat and book, the jester with his cap and bells, and the gentlemen and their ladies. How the craftsmen must have enjoyed their work.

Outside is the Saint's stone, a huge granite boulder, broken in two. The legend is that St Levan sat on the rock when resting from fishing, and one day made this prophecy when he broke it with his staff:

> When with panniers astride
> A pack horse can ride,
> Through St Levan's stone.
> The world will be done.

Reverend Maurice Friggens, who has the three lovely churches of St Buryan, Sennen and St Levan in his care, told me: 'The gap is supposed to be widening ever so slowly. It is taking a very long time—and that is very reassuring.' Between the church and the beach is the holy well and remains of an old chapel.

St Mary the Virgin Church at **Penzance** was consecrated less than 150 years ago, with the work of 'Newlyn School' artist, Ernest Proctor, very much in evidence at the high altar and canopy. At the altar is the painting of Mary with the Christ Child and St John, and there is more than a colourful flourish of originality and eccentricity in the spectacular Penzance skyline scene of church and Lloyd's Bank, painted to mark the church's centenary in the 1930s.

Just as Penzance had its 'mother church' at Madron in the old days, so **Newlyn** was part of the parish of Madron and Paul, with a new parish cut out in 1848. The church is comparatively young, and well worth seeing, particularly for the work of sculptor-vicar Reverend Alan Wyon, and the reredos in terracotta representing The Last Supper.

We all like to believe that the people of Mount's Bay were the first on the English

A fair fills up the spare space at Penzance harbour, with the church in the background.

The approach to St Peter's Square at Newlyn around 1903.

mainland to learn of the death of Nelson and of his victory at Trafalgar in 1805. The Mayor of Penzance, Thomas Giddy, announced the news and led a procession to the town's mother church of **Madron**. A banner, improvised for the occasion, still leads the way at the annual Trafalgar Day Sunday service here. It bears the words: 'Mourn for the Brave, the Immortal Nelson's Gone. His last sea fight is Fought, His work of Glory done.' It has a place of pride in this treasure church, with its links stretching back down the centuries.

Hanging from a wooden frame is the bell from 'Ding Dong' mine which closed in 1878, there is a fourteenth-century panel of ten angels—among the best examples of English alabaster work—and the first Mayor, John Maddern, who died in 1621 is remembered on a slate panel.

In the old days this was the mother church of Penzance and the leading families are remembered around the walls. Curiously enough, it was another Maddern who gave his name to the church and village, St Maddern, who came in the sixth century. The wishing well, and his Baptistry, still used for baptisms, must not be missed.

Paul Church, up the hill from Mousehole, was destroyed by fire when the Spaniards came raiding in 1595. It still has the cannon balls to prove it, and the armour of Squire William Godolphin who died in 1689. The tale of the 'invasion' and burning was retold in 1980 when the Spanish Ambassador in London sent £50 which was he said 'purely symbolic' towards the cost of repairs to the church roof!

Inside the church is a unique memorial. It

is to the eight men of the Penlee lifeboat *Solomon Browne* who gave their lives in attempting to save the eight on the coaster *Union Star* in December 1981. This is a granite boulder, weighing a ton, brought from Lamorna Cove close to where the lifeboat was lost, with a 'ship's lantern' on top, and a glass crystal chalice inside inscribed with the lifeboatmen's initials.

It was to this church that the Duke and Duchess of Kent came in 1982 to join the remembrance service for the men of Penlee. The invasion and the Penlee tragedy span the centuries, but in January 1942 the church windows were damaged by German bombs.

St Hilary was no Irishman, but a Frenchman who was Bishop of Poitiers in the fourth century. This church was consecrated in 1855 after most of the original was destroyed in a fire. Many remember the troubles in the 1930s between the Kensitites and Father Bernard Walke, but much restoration has taken place in recent years. There is a great deal to admire including a rare statue of St Joseph, at least 300 years old, and the painting in the reredos is ascribed to a fifteenth-century artist.

Scenes from the lives of the Cornish Saints have been painted by members of that celebrated Newlyn School, and the church is filled with delightful 'modern' works of art such as the large crucifix by Phyllis Yglesias—one of the two sisters who founded the Mousehole bird hospital. But there is also the ancient Constantine Stone, a relic of Roman occupation, dated 307 AD, and outside is the mysterious 'Noti Noti' stone. What does it mean?

It was just over one-hundred years ago that **Marazion** became a separate parish from St Hilary and the present building—covering the site of the older church—was consecrated in 1861. Certain to interest is the low rail

Perranuthnoe Church is dedicated to the Patron
Saint of miners. *Above*: the stamps at Lower Quarter,
Ludgvan about 1905-10. *Right*: West Cornwall
miners with donkey shay. *Far right*: The medieval
wall painting at Breage Church.

around the war memorial across the main
road from the church entrance, for this metal-
work includes six bars of music, and the
words 'Abide with Me: Fast Falls the Even-
tide'. These remind us that Reverend Henry
Francis Lyte, the writer of this famous hymn,
ministered here in the early nineteenth
century.

Perranuthnoe Church is dedicated to St
Piran, the Patron Saint of Cornish Miners, and
the visitor must look for his figure on the
reredos, a lovely example of craftsmanship.
His hand is on the millstone on which, according to legend, he sailed from Ireland to
Cornwall. There are also some 'fragments' of
the first church here in 1160 including the
granite Norman font with its carvings.
Nearby and over the door is a small round
ancient stone carving of St James holding a
staff.

Germoe is held to be a name of a King—
his sister was St Breage—who landed near
Hayle estuary with the Irish missionaries.

They lived close to one another, and he was probably buried here. Like so many others, this has its origin in a Norman church—the twelfth century was a busy building time in Cornwall—and there are many remains including a Norman stoup which had probably been walled in when the Parliamentarians threatened to visit and was rediscovered in 1860.

The mystery of the 'Germoe monkeys' is bound to tease. On each side of the outer door are carvings of these long-tailed monkeys, recognisable despite the years and the weather. Experts believe that the medieval sculptor put them here to represent the 'spirit of evil and mischief' driven from the building.

The ancient font is of pre-Conquest date, and possibly from the original small stone church. Out in the north-east corner of the churchyard is the fascinating St Germoe's Chair, used in the Palm Sunday celebrations of the old church.

The medieval wall paintings of **Breage** were lost from view for generations following the fanatical efforts of the Puritan movement, and it was less than one-hundred years ago that they were rediscovered. It is believed they were painted soon after the church was completed, around 1470, and include St Christopher carrying the Christchild, a ten foot high figure of 'Christ of the Trades', St Hilary and St Corentine. These are in the north aisle, while in the south are some others including a figure of a king in the coronation robe of ermine and holding an orb, which was discovered as recently as 1955. A real effort is being made to raise funds to restore these wall paintings to their former splendour.

Another feature of the church, and tucked away in a corner, is a Roman milestone which bears the name of Marcus Cassianus Postumus, who was Emperor of Gaul from 260–268. It is the only stone bearing his name known to exist in Britain.

A popular corner of old Porthleven—Pascoe's teahouse.

Porthleven harbour (*top*) around 1880 with Buenos Aires Row in the background. This terrace was demolished in 1889 and was still inhabited when the photograph was taken. *Above*: Gunwalloe Church in the 1930s.

Don't forget to look up or you will miss the medieval helmets of the Godolphin family suspended from the roof.

St Bartholomew's Church at **Porthleven** is very modern by comparison—dedicated in 1842—but here there is a magnificent wooden 'Hanging Rood', anchor-shaped. A gift of Squire Rogers in 1919, it has the Crucified Lord in the central span, with the mourning women on each side. There is a screen and pulpit of finely wrought iron, and in four of the windows are Christ and the Madonna, with Barnabas and Bartholomew.

Marconi's face on the Old Inn sign gazes down opposite **Mullion** Church which has beautiful fifteenth-century oak seats, carved perhaps from timber of an ancient forest at Goonhilly Downs. There are the 'Instruments

Two gems from the photographic archives. *Above*:
The ladies are wearing splendid hats at Mullion
about 1910.

Right: Artists at the entrance to the cave at Mullion
Cove, probably in the 1890s.

of the Passion', including pincers and spear, the crown of thorns, the nails, the scourge, dice and torches in an impressive show. There is an unusual medieval side-on view of Jonah in the belly of the whale.

The church also has the unique feature of a 'dog door' in its old main south door. 'I think it comes from a time when the economy of the area was based on the sheep, and the dogs came with the shepherd, and could leave when they wanted to,' the Vicar, Reverend P. H. Thompson, told me. Don't forget the very old north door, of oak with wooden studs, and thought to be eleventh-century or earlier.

Gunwalloe Church has been fighting against sea and sand for years, and still survives. The spray flies over it, and the sea laps this precious building, in danger of being left on an island with cliff erosion.

Inside are two pieces of the sixteenth-century rood screen, made from the wood of a ship wrecked here in 1526 on its way from Flanders to Portugal. There are two painted panels, each of four Apostles, including Matthew, John and James, which were restored a few years ago. An unusual feature is its detached west bell tower, perhaps thirteenth century, built into the rock.

Cury might well have been the setting for

the first English services in Cornwall, and on your arrival look up at the Norman doorway with its chain of endless rings for Eternal Life. There is an old pulpit at the west end, and an ancient alms box looking the worst for wear, but most visitors will be fascinated by a peephole and a carving. For there is a 'leper squint' to the altar, and two little narrow staircases, while on the north wall is a grotesque head with an open mouth showing teeth and tongue!

You must be prepared for the unexpected in our churches, but I never expected to see angels dancing the 'Furry Dance'. There they were, in stained glass, above the altar and the mosaic reredos of the Last Supper, tripping along holding aloft the 'Hal-an-Tow' branches. What a picture for **Helston** Parish Church, built in the mid-eighteenth century.

Ruan Major bench-ends and part of rood screen in Landewednack Church at Lizard Churchtown in 1922.

They dance merrily—the wings appear to be no handicap—with the music on scrolls between them in a lovely east window. The arms of the Godolphin family are also here, for the church was the gift of the Earl of Godolphin, including the great chandelier. Many changes have been made in recent years, including the removal of the gallery, and it is worth looking for the framed monumental brasses in the north porch and the framed letter to Earl Godolphin in praise of his generosity.

It is worth a diversion to the farming village of **Sithney** if only for two features. In the church there are six portraits, in glass by thirteenth-century artists, of four women saints and two men with beards. These are from the previous church on this site, as is the statuette of St Sithney beneath the south east pinnacle of the tower. He is believed to have been buried here.

The sea is always with us at **Lizard** Church, and around are the graves of wrecked mariners and drowned fishermen. Even one of the Rectors was drowned, Henry Tonkin Coulson, in 1840, while bathing at Kilcobben Cove, 'when his health promised a long period of usefulness', as his memorial declares.

The celebrated message of King Charles I to the church of Cornwall has a prominent place on a large wooden board put up in 1829.

Tradition has it that the last sermon in the Cornish language was preached here by Reverend Francis Robinson in 1670, but you can go back to the time of Agincourt for the Rector of 1404 whose name is included in the words in Latin on the font, 'Master Richard Bolham made me'.

Make a point of looking for the six-hundred-year-old bell, among the oldest pre-Reformation bells in Cornwall, now kept inside the church, and you are certain to admire the serpentine pulpit which demonstrates the craftsmanship of this area.

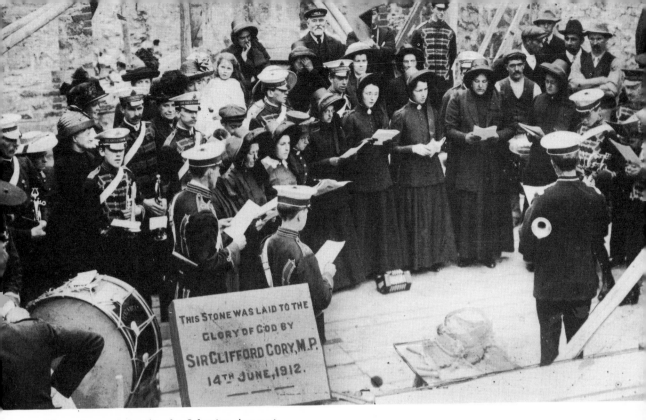

THIS STONE WAS LAID TO THE GLORY OF GOD BY SIR CLIFFORD CORY, M.P. 14TH JUNE, 1912.

Above: **A proud day for the Salvation Army at Penzance in 1912 at the stone-laying in Queen Street.** *Below*: **Harvest festival at the Salvation Army.**

7

A Cruel Shore: Wreckers and Smugglers

Curiously enough, the passage of time has allowed a barrier to be built between the legends and harsh realities of the wreckers and smugglers of Mount's Bay. To the evil wreckers has come rigid condemnation and to the 'gallant' smugglers the colourful myths of romance, yet both were involved in the harsh struggles of life and death.

We like to think that every harbour had its tunnel leading up through the village to the fishermen's backyards. My own family believe that one was at the back of my grandfather's cottage on Newlyn Cliff. When excavation work was carried out at New Street in Penzance a few years back a large tunnel was disclosed, and there are many similar tales of smugglers' 'hiding holes' being discovered. Two caves were found, close to the churchyard at Wendron during rebuilding.

Whether smuggler or wrecker there was always the battle of wits in the struggle for survival. The Customs men and the coastguards waged war to keep the brandy and the 'baccy from coming ashore. Mount's Bay was far from the Channel Islands and from France: it was also far from the law. There were no real roads, justice was a long time a-coming along those lonely bridle paths.

At times there was collusion between smugglers and officers: at one Cornish port three chief officers in succession were dismissed under circumstances that point that way. Let no-one dispute the talents of the local men. 'The coasts here swarm with smugglers' wrote a Penzance agent in the 1750s asking for troops to be stationed in the district and particularly at Helston. He declared that a Dutch ship, laden with claret was wrecked near Helston, and 'in twenty-four hours the tinners cleared all'.

At the other end of the spectrum there was tragedy. In 1822 crew and cargo were lost when the *Rose* was wrecked near St Michael's Mount. Fifteen years later the *Friends* was lost near Wherrytown, Penzance...with almost all fifty seven kegs of spirits recovered by the coastguard.

Whenever the smuggler was toasted in best brandy the talk must have turned to John Carter, most famed of them all, thanks mainly to the writings of his brother. John was known as the 'King of Prussia' because, as a boy when playing at soldiers, he would always claim to play the role of Frederick the Great. He ended up by giving his name to his home, Prussia Cove.

On one occasion the Excise officers took his cargo and stored it at the custom house at Penzance, but his reputation was at stake for he had to keep his word—and his order—to a customer. That night the honest smuggler broke open the custom store with his armed men and took his own goods. When the officers discovered the loss next morning, they realised it was John Carter: no other cargo had been touched.

One celebrated day, having built a battery of some small cannon at his home, he opened fire on the revenue sloop *Fairy* which was chasing a smuggler's boat into the cove. The sloop withdrew, but next day mounted soldiers arrived with their muskets—but 'The King' seems to have got away with it again.

John's brother, Captain Harry, wrote an autobiography which told of his lively years, and then of his conversion to the Wesleyans—he spent the last thirty years quietly at Rinsey, preaching and farming.

He worked as a miner from nine until he was seventeen, then went to sea, learning to read and write and keep his own accounts. He did so well that in his twenties he had a new eighteen-ton sloop built, and, as he put it, went on for many years 'sinning and repenting'.

His relations with the Collector of Customs at Penzance was so strong that he was once asked to pursue a privateer, the *Black Prince* from Dunkirk. 'It was not a very agreeable business,' he remarked, but he did not want to offend the Collector.

The 'trade' had an ideal corner at Mullion, and there is one story of a group of smugglers being taken by surprise by the crew of a

Crabpots line the path at Prussia Cove—home of the smuggler John Carter—pictured in the 1890s.

gun-brig, only for their vessel to be 're-possessed' when the locals returned fully armed.

Perhaps the story of 'brandy for the parson' had its origin when Reverend Thomas Whitford of Cury was found with four casks from the *Lady Lucy*, wrecked at Gunwalloe in 1739.

Smugglers were also double agents, and the Emperor Napoleon remarked: 'during the war all the information I received came through the smugglers. They are people who have courage and ability to do anything for money.'

There was little mercy when they were caught. In 1830 two boats out of Tresco, the *Speedwell* and the *Mary Ann*, were arrested on having been seen at Roscoff, and running

their cargoes at the Land's End and Mount's Bay. They were convicted and the boats condemned to be cut up.

'O Lord, we pray thee not that wrecks should happen but that if wrecks do happen Thou wilt guide them in to the Isles of Scilly for the benefit of the poor inhabitants,' (A Cornish 'Amen' to that.)

The wreckers may be thought of as 'human vultures' and their reputation at the time was fearsome. 'They'll cut a large trading vessel to pieces in one tide, and cut everybody that offers to oppose them,' wrote one contemporary. 'I have seen many a poor man half-dead cast ashore and crawling out of the reach of the waves, fallen upon, and in a manner stripped naked by these villains.'

Some believed the gentry joined in the shares. John Wesley described it as 'the scandal of Cornwall' which the gentry could prevent whenever they pleased. Another distinguished man, Walter Borlase, declared: 'Are there in that country no Justices? Where

The crew was rescued but the *Taycraig* sank in 1936. She dragged her anchors in a gale and ended up at the Gear Pole. St Mary's Church, Penzance, stands out in the background.

The steamer *Brankelow* went ashore near Gunwalloe in April 1890, along the coast from where HMS *Anson* was wrecked off Loe Bar in 1807.

were they when the laws were violated in so daring a manner?'

The wreckers who plundered the vessels that had the great misfortune to strike the Cornish rocks were often half-starved, illiterate ruffians. When a ship went ashore at Marazion just before Christmas 1749 it was plundered 'by the barbarians of Breage and Germoe'.

It needed three important developments to bring an end to the worst of these evils: the influence of Methodism, better living standards and a new coastguard service.

A rapier was kept at Castle Horneck, given to Captain Samuel Borlase by merchants from Boston 'for bravely keeping the tinners from plundering their ship stranded in Mounts Bay' in 1763.

Today we hear no stories of wrecking and few of smuggling in Mount's Bay, but there is still a busy HM Custom and Excise 'Custom House' at Dock Lane, Penzance, with ships' Masters and Agents coming to report to the 'Long Room'. It has stood on the site for over two hundred years.

'Penzance covers a district from Lizard Point around Land's End, almost to Perranporth,' the Senior Officer, Mr Tony Groves explained to me, 'and there is a twenty-four-hour cover day in, week out.' In the old days many of the villages had their own custom house.

These days the summertime yachts in the ports and harbours make plenty of work, with checks and documents, and there is always the watch for drugs. 'We have had them in the past, and there is no doubt we shall have some in the future—it is our job to try and find out,' he commented.

'Two or three years ago a fishing boat brought in a load of cannabis which was landed here at Penzance. It was a British boat, with a ton of cannabis hidden under the fish, and they were caught at a later date by a combined police and Customs operation in another part of the country.

'The opportunities for smugglers are enormous, but it is our job to try and stop them. If you have a success you know about it. If

1910 in Newlyn. *Left:* **Trewarveneth Street.** *Below:* **Newlyn slip. The narrow streets and back to back cottages gave good cover to the smugglers.** *Right:* **The Strand at Newlyn and the rocks where the fish market stands today.**

you don't…then you don't know what you have missed. This is one of the infuriating parts of our job.'

There is no Revenue cutter today but there is a Custom and Excise launch which makes frequent visits to this area. Mount's Bay might lack the excitement of the old times, but the vigilance has to be equally as keen.

Do not fear you contemporary mariner—remember Preben Peterson? He was the bearded Dane with the magnificent yacht *Esperanca* that went on the rocks of Porthgwarra while sailing from Brazil to Copenhagen just a few years ago. Without a proper chart, and very tired after long hours of watch, he fell asleep and didn't know where he was when he came aground. He thought he might be at the Lizard, but far from hitting wreckers and smugglers, Preben fell among friends.

There were two holes in the ferro-concrete hull, and all seemed lost, but local farmers rallied to the cause and finally floated her clear with bouyant plastic drums. It was a time of helping and of friendships—everyone seemed the better for it—and Preben, with his lovely wife and son, was most grateful. 'We slept in their beds, we dined at their tables, and have been looked after like we were at the Hilton Hotel,' he told me.

The boat came to Newlyn, then to Penzance pier where the repair work went on for months, and one friend he had made, Richard Hills, kept Preben company all the way to Copenhagen when the *Esperanca* was ship-shape again.

This is the perfect answer to all those who believe the old lamp still flickers on the clifftop, and that fishermen, farmers and tinners wait their chance to plunder.

Fishing has always been one of the main occupations of Mount's Bay. *Above left*: These old salts are believed to be Porthleven fishermen in Newlyn harbour. *Below left*: Landing the pilchards—'unmaicing' the silver shoal from the nets of PZ30. *Below*: Making and preparing the baskets for the fish catch.

8

Men in a Million

No man has made a deeper impression on me than Group Captain Cheshire VC, a war hero who has devoted his life for forty years to the incurably sick.

Cheshire Homes are now world-wide, and Mount's Bay played an important part in that venture, first at Predannack and then at Long Rock. The aim is to give the patients a full life, to make them feel they have a contribution to make, and to let them know they belong to a family.

The generosity of the St Levan family brought the St Teresa's Home at Long Rock, opened by Lord Denning, in 1956. When I last saw him in 1983 Leonard Cheshire was frail and tired, but his vision as clear as ever,

Porthleven harbour in 1903. It was here that Wing Commander Guy Gibson spent his summer holidays as a child.

Group Captain Leonard Cheshire, second from left, at St Teresa's Home at Long Rock, with the Dowager Lady St Levan (*left*) and Lord and Lady St Levan.

his purpose as single-minded. 'No county in England has shown the widespread spirit of support that Cornwall has,' he told me. 'In a certain sense I have always thought that our foundation began here.'

After the war he came to Cornwall with Barnes Wallis to work on the swing-wing 'plane experiment. 'Suddenly we got an application from an epileptic, a strong fit boy.

'So I invited him here and it all really grew from that.' Cheshire took one of the old empty buildings at the Predannack airfield— for nothing—put the boy to work, and helped him and got others to assist.

Did Cheshire's wartime experiences—he flew as an observer on the Atom Bomb mission to Japan—lead him to this work? 'They led me in the direction of feeling that, having fought such a dreadful war that cost so many lives, fifty million, one owed some duty to work in one way or another for peace.' How deep a part does his personal faith play in this? 'I think it is the foundation on which everything else rests. Without that, I think probably my course would have wobbled a bit.'

The day when the Grand Fleet came to Mount's Bay in 1904, a magnificent sight.

The NATO fleet came to the bay in 1947 and repeated the picture of over forty years before.

Two other wartime heroes have a close link with Mount's Bay. One of the most celebrated was Wing Commander Guy Gibson whose gallantry and daring deeds earned him the Victoria Cross, DSO and DFC. This ace pilot has a road named after him at Porthleven, for it was here that he spent many happy holidays as a child with his grandparents Captain and Mrs Strike, at Breageside.

It is 'Gibson Way' and one of the residents, Mr Alfred Richards, not only remembers playing with Guy as a lad, but called his own son Gibson Richards. There was even talk at one time of putting up a memorial in the town to the 'Dam Busters' hero, whose mother came from Porthleven, and there is a brass plaque and his photograph in the WI Hall.

The other, born and bred in Newlyn, Lieutenant Bob Davies, saved St Paul's Cathedral from an unexploded bomb during the 1940 blitz on London. The George Cross he received was sold in 1983 for £16,000. It was awarded for 'unremitting bravery' in defusing the bomb which fell in Dean's Yard on 12 September. He died in Australia in 1975. Bob, who lived at Trewarveneth Street, has many relatives in the district, although he did not spend many of his adult years in the village.

Very few Mount's Bay men have worn the Victoria Cross. Joe Trewavas of Mousehole was the first. When Victoria, then a young Queen of thirty eight, first presented the VC in Hyde Park almost one hundred and thirty years ago, he was the ninth hero in line. Curiously enough, his home village has no memorial to his achievements during the seige of Sebastapol.

Joe was a splendid figure of a young naval seaman when he served in the Black Sea. With two hundred enemy soldiers firing at him from less than one hundred yards away, he risked his life in cutting adrift a pontoon bridge in the Azov Sea. He was wounded in helping his comrades, and stopping the enemy advance that day, just a year after the Charge of the Light Brigade.

When he came home after his discharge from the Navy in 1862 he had a clutch of medals as well as the VC. There was the Conspicuous Gallantry Medal, the French Legion of Honour, the Crimean and Turkish medals, and several bars. He rarely wore his medals or spoke of his deeds. He bought a boat, went fishing, married and had two sons and two daughters. In typically modest Cornish style he didn't talk overmuch about his personal achievements, nor of his courage, spirit and heroism on that July day, nor of his service in the West Indies and New Zealand.

A lifelong believer in 'peaceful persuasion' was William Lovett the Chartist, who was born in Newlyn and spent his life's energy on behalf of the working class. 'His main achievement was in working to get the vote for men,' said Mr John Beckerlegge to me one day at his Keigwin Manor home. 'He was anxious at

Cornwall's first Victoria Cross winner in 1856—Joe Trewavas of Mousehole.

first to include suffrage for women as well, but he was advised that it would be easier to get it passed if his appeal was simply for men. Today there are many people who will not trouble to vote and are half-hearted.'

No vote—no musket, was the call. 'He said why should men be wanted for the army when they were not wanted to govern the country, and he even went to prison for his principles.' Because he was a Chartist he was looked upon as an undesirable sort of person by the Government.

Lovett was before his country, and before his day. Later he devoted his time to social conditions and the poor, particularly in the workhouse, and ran Sunday schools teaching arithmetic, writing, reading and general education.

In a grave near the war memorial in the village of St Erth lies the body of a remarkable soldier. Little is known of Lieutenant Herbert Carter, born in 1874, whose father was for many years Vicar of the parish.

In 1904 a group of British soldiers unexpectedly encountered 3,000 of the Mullah's men in Somaliland, East Africa. After charging the enemy twice the British had to retire, but Lieutenant Carter saw one of his colleagues, a Sikh, lying on the ground surrounded by about twenty of the enemy, and being pricked by their spears. He charged the Dervishes, and fired at their leader who fell. During this lull he made three unsuccessful attempts to fix the unconscious Sikh across his saddle. The fourth time he was able to gallop through a

The thatched cottage has gone, and now, on the right is the entrance to the Newlyn Centenary Methodist Church. Pictured in 1910, it was an earlier Newlyn that William Lovett, the Chartist, knew.

hail of bullets, one of which pierced his helmet. He brought the man away from the Dervishes, and for his conspicuous bravery was awarded the Victoria Cross.

Everyone knows of Bob Fitzsimmons. Wasn't he the only Cornish-born fighter to win the heavyweight championship of the World? Yet how little is known of his life and boxing career by most local sportsmen. He had the longest career of any official world-title holder with over thirty-two years, from 1882 to 1914. He won his last world title in his forty-second year in California in 1903.

It all began way back on 26 May in 1863 when he was born in Wendron Street, Helston. His father was borough constable, and his mother Jane had the maiden name of Strongman, perfect for a future champion. Although locals signed a petition asking Mr and Mrs Fitzsimmons not to leave Helston they went and settled in New Zealand. Bob grew strong from blacksmith's work, from swinging a sledge hammer at a foundry, and claimed that he started fighting bare-knuckled from the age of fifteen. Never a giant heavyweight in size, Bob had huge shoulders and chest, and a slim waist. Success carried him to Australia and then America.

He beat Jack Dempsey in January 1891 for the middleweight championship, and went on to defeat such legends as James J. Corbett and James J. Jefferies. Bob won three world titles at different weights, had a lively theatrical career, married four times, and fought his last title fight when he was forty six, meeting Bill Lang for the Australian heavyweight crown in 1909.

He came back to England that same year, although there is no record of a visit home to Helston, and he died of pneumonia on 22 October in 1917 in Chicago—and he was only fifty four.

Look around Helston and the Lizard Peninsula and you will see many links with Gugliemo Marconi, the Italian who heralded a revolution in communications. This genius is remembered with a 'twin town' link with Sasso Marconi and Helston, an Inn sign, a road name, as well as that monument at Poldhu unveiled in November 1937, four months after his death.

The earliest Transatlantic signal was the letter 'S' in morse, sent from Poldhu and received in Newfoundland in December 1901. It has a place in history, and one man who can remember Marconi at work is seventy-eight-year-old Mr John C. Corin of Coverack, 'It is astonishing what achievements in communication have come since that first signal,' he remarked. He can recall those fragile aerials into the sky and the working huts nearby.

He was just a young boy when he saw the great man come ashore from the yacht *Elettra*. Marconi would—of all things when one realises the situation today—go to the Coverack post office to use the telephone!

He chose Poldhu as the site for his wireless station, powerful enough to span the Atlantic, with an uninterrupted path for the radio waves across the ocean…and seclusion. After the first signal Poldhu still played a major part in radio communication, being a commercial station from 1905–22, and in the 1920s the signals were used to test out his short-wave system while he sailed in the Atlantic and Mediterranean on his yacht. It was closed in 1934.

Not everyone thought well of Marconi, however. Over at Newlyn and Mousehole the fishermen blamed him, and his aerials, for the perpetual rain that kept falling and the gales that kept blowing, and prepared a petition against this new-fangled science!

Few men are held in greater esteem at Helston than Henry Trengrouse, 1772–1854. His gravestone, with its nautical motif outside the front entrance of Helston Church, tells the story. He was a man 'who profoundly impressed by the great loss of life by shipwreck, rendered most signal service to humanity by devoting the greater portion of his life and means to the invention of the "Rocket Apparatus", for communicating between

A quiet moment off Poldhu in 1904, with Signor
Marconi in the boat with Mr Kemp (listening with
headphones) conducting directional experiments
with horizontal wires. The aerial was supported by
cork floats astern of the boat.

stranded ships and the shore, whereby many thousands of lives have been saved.'

Helston Museum gives him a place of honour with his original 'Bosun's Chair' and lifejacket 'Sailor's Life-Spencer', both of which he designed.

A local cabinet maker, he had been appalled by the tragedy of HMS *Anson*, and began to work on ship-to-shore lifesaving equipment which could be used by shipwrecked sailors. In 1807, just after Christmas, the *Anson* was wrecked on Loe Bar, and more than one hundred men were drowned as they tried to swim the short distance to shore.

You cannot escape the watchful gaze of Sir Humphry Davy at Penzance. Contemplating his glorious achievements, and with a hand resting on a miner's safety lamp, he commands Market Jew Street, with the same assurance as he commanded the scientific life of this country in the early 1800s.

Penzance is proud of him—he was born just a few steps away from this statue—and he made the occasional visit back to his home town after leaving for fame and fortune. His father was a wood carver of Varfell, Ludgvan and Penzance, and his mother was a Millett of St Just, but he died with his inscription in Latin on his tomb far away: 'Here lies Humphry Davy, Knight Baronet of Great

The young and handsome Humphry Davy from an original by Sir Thomas Lawrence in the possession of the Royal Society. His statue stands at the top of Market Jew Street in Penzance, pictured below before the age of the motor-car.

Britain. Investigator extraordinary into the secrets of nature. Born at Penzance among the Cornish in December 1778. Died at Geneva, among the Swiss 29th May, 1829.'

So much achieved, yet burnt out at fifty. As a lad he fished from Penzance pier for grey mullet, and one of his last books, written while seeking to restore his strength was *Days of Fly Fishing*.

He lived and worked at a time when an intelligent man's interest could embrace science and the arts: he was seven times President of the Royal Society—for the first time at the age of forty one—and was a friend of the poet Coleridge and novelist Walter Scott.

I like to think the place where he conducted his first experiments is still with us at Penzance, for tradition has it that Peasgoods Pharmacy, close to that ever-present statue, was the building where he became apprenticed to chemist and surgeon Mr Bingham Borlase in February 1795. There is still a little room upstairs where the apprentices slept.

His fame as a lecturer, his isolation of the elements, potassium and sodium, his election as the youngest Fellow of the Royal Society at twenty five, all added to his stature. We remember him most for his invention of the safety lamp at a time when coal mines were going deeper and disaster and danger rapidly increasing. Sir Humphry, who lived in the

Celebrations at Wherrytown, Penzance, at the end of the 1914-18 war.

dawn of a new age, said that his sole object was 'to serve the cause of humanity'. His final visit to Penzance came in 1821 when he was honoured by a public dinner.

It has always struck me as remarkable that, in the span of some twenty years, West Cornwall was 'home' for a time at least to three of the most original minds of this and any century.

At Porthcurno the philosopher Bertrand Russell spent months at a time, in the 1920s at Zennor lived the novelist and poet D. H. Lawrence until driven out by the wartime rumour-mongers of 1917, while to Polgigga and then Mousehole came the beautiful Welsh poet Dylan Thomas.

It was in 1936 that Dylan came to Polgigga—with the nearest pub miles away—and when his host Mrs Wyn Henderson moved to Mousehole so did he, and described it as 'the loveliest village in England'.

That year he met Caitlin Macnamara in London, in the summer of 1937 they came to Cornwall, and on 12 July were married at Penzance register office, going to live for a time at Newlyn, 'where gulls fly in to breakfast'. One Penzance man who knew him well at this time was journalist Joe Martin whose first memory of him at Polgigga was of his 'curls like a cherub and what looked like a cherub's nose as well'.

Those were the days before his tremendous fame. He lived up the steep Raginnis Hill, a daily walk and exercise described by him as 'Raginnis-is-good-for-you Hill'. It was Ethel who then commanded 'The Ship Inn' magnificently. Dylan would make for the room on the left, and usually the table at the far end, with his sense of mischief not far below the surface of the air of innocence.

'There was a night when Dylan lit a small bonfire inside the right-hand pocket of my coat while we sat opposite each other,' recalls his friend. 'So absorbed was he in his act of incendiarism that I became absorbed myself and it was not until smoke curled up that I showed any alarm. With exemplary presence of mind Dylan picked up a glass, probably mine, and emptied it into the pocket which I then turned inside out.'

They really drank very little, and Dylan had a special word of thanks when Joe wrote a few lines about him in *The Cornishman*: 'It was the first thing about me to be published in the news columns of a newspaper,' he said. Joe met Dylan and Caitlin on that wedding day. He jumped off the bus at Mousehole to find them waiting to jump on.

'They said they were going to get married and begged me to go back with them to the Register Office. Apparently Wyn had given them the money for the licence and now they urgently needed witnesses and moral support. But there were times when I had work to do, and this was one of them as I tried to explain before the bus moved off.' What a moment to miss.

Fishing was not the only occupation of the Bay
(*right*). *Above*: The blacksmith preparing for work.
Below: Cunnack's Tanyard at St John's, Helston, in
1883. In the top hat is Mr George James Cunnack,
1823-1911; while on the left is Mr Francis Henry
Cunnack, 1861-1936. The Tanyard was demolished
in 1968 during road widening.

From horse and sail to the motor engine. *Above*:
'Jersey Cars' leave Penzance for Land's End. *Below*:
The three-masted barque *W. W. McLaughlan* built
in 1891 in New Brunswick, pictured in Penzance
harbour about 1900.

Above: **Outside Hill's Hotel—the Three Tuns—at Lizard Churchtown about 1903.** *Below*: **A view of the Godolphin Hotel at Marazion in the years between the wars.**

9

Ancient ... and Modern

The silhouette of the mine stack and engine house, the lonely wayside cross, the crooked standing stone that surprise in West Penwith, are no longer taken for granted. Today, more than ever, they are named, listed and protected.

Our geological history has provided some astonishing contrasts, from the grey 'Cornish' granite of Land's End peninsula to the killas of Mount's Bay and the serpentine of the Lizard. So, too, has human progress, for earliest man with his worshipping and burial stones to the spectacular satellite aerials of Goonhilly, and the continuous and parallel exploitation of tin and copper over thousands of years.

There is a treasure chest of antiquities, churchyard and hedgerow house our Celtic crosses, some still startlingly 'alive', such as at Boskenna and the market cross of Penzance, now outside Penlee House.

In Madron parish is the Baptistry and wishing well, still believed to have curative powers by many, as the pieces of cloth tied to the bushes will testify. The nearby 'holed stone', the Men-an-Tol, is a prized relic. Did it mark a tomb—can sick people still be cured by crawling through? Also in this parish is the Men Scryfa, the 'inscribed stone'... was it

Left: **An old Cornish cross at Boskenna near St Buryan.** *Right*: **This eleventh-century cross was outside the Market House at Penzance from 1867-99. Believed to be the cross of King Ricatus, it is today outside the Penlee House Museum.**

A scene including shire horse and stone circle. The Merry Maidens between Lamorna and St Buryan—they were turned to stone for dancing on the Sabbath.

Ryalvran, son of Kenwal, who died here in battle?

Perhaps much of the pleasure lies in the mystery as that of the nineteen 'Merry Maidens' on the road between Lamorna and St Buryan. We all like the legend of the girls being turned into granite stones after dancing on the Sabbath in 2400 BC!

Ritual and ceremony had much to do with this monument, no doubt, as at the stone circle at Boscawen-Un, a few miles away. The scene came to life again with the first modern Gorsedd of Cornwall, and its golden jubilee in 1978.

Amidst the rare flowers at Goonhilly are the sites of three separate Celtic villages, barrows and standing stones, one of which—of serpentine—almost fifteen foot high, now stands on the St Keverne side of the satellite station. Kynance—it means 'gorge'—was occupied for thousands of years, with domestic pottery from the Bronze Age being discovered here and remains of the later Iron Age Celts.

Lanyon Quoit, at Madron, with its granite slab over seventeen feet long perched on three standing stones, is believed to be the site of a 2000 BC tomb, but it was rebuilt in 1824 after collapsing. It previously had four 'legs'. The barrow mounds were burial places for our Bronze Age ancestors, over 1000 BC, and can be spotted through the district, particularly at Tregiffian, St Buryan.

The ancient settlement of Chysauster, near Gulval, is the finest example locally of our Celtic ancestors in Roman times, with their characteristic oval courtyard house, fogou and fields. At Treryn Dinas, St Levan, is the largest of our cliff castles.

A visitor could spend an absorbing week tracking down this story of our past—and I am sure many local people would be the wiser for deepening their knowledge of the rich history that lies around us.

We call it the 'Newlyn School' but I don't remember there being a Newlyn man or woman among the artists. Harold Harvey, however, one of the second generation of painters, was born at Penzance and spent much of his life at Newlyn. They were not from the village, and when at last there was an art gallery many of them had gone their several ways, but they brought fame to themselves and to the little fishing community.

Before the turn of the century, mainly from 1882, the artists came to paint in the open air and to picture the local people at work, at play, celebrating and mourning. They found hard-working honest folk who gained pride in being at the centre of attention, with fisherman John Henry Tonkin in 'The Lighthouse' and Robert Hitchens the groom in 'Health of the Bride'.

Their leader Stanhope Forbes, known as 'Daddy Forbes' to local people in the later years, was most revered.

This 'Plein Air School' came in a flood to Newlyn, and the artists with their canvasses and easels could be found in many streets and piers up until the 1940s. The Rue de Beaux Arts in Trewarveth Street, Malt House, Wheal Betsy, Bellevue and Faughan, are places that will always be associated with this energetic young group who thirsted for recognition and fame in their art, and revelled in entertainment together on stage as a hobby.

Some painters of 'The Newlyn School' in the 1880s. Seated, on the right, is the 'Father' of the School, Stanhope Forbes. Standing, left to right: Frank Bodilly, Fred Millard, Frank Bramley, William Blandford Fletcher, William Breakespeare, Ralph Todd, Alexander Chevalier Tayler, Henry Scott Tuke. Seated: William Wainwright, Edwin Harris.

Forbes, who was ninety when he died in 1947, and was unquestionably the leader from the earliest days, wrote: 'Here every corner was a picture, and more important from the point of view of the figure-painter, the people seemed to fall naturally into their places, and to harmonise with their surroundings.'

I remember as a schoolboy model going to Faughan when he was in his eighties, some fifty-five years after the success of 'A Fish Sale on a Cornish Beach' at the Royal Academy in 1885. A lean, white-haired old man, still painting busily.

From his school in The Meadow, and from the appreciation of art that developed, has come a local tradition of our own time and modern style. Jack Pender, Michael Praed and Margo Maeckelberghe, are three who have a fine reputation, and the granite Art Gallery, under the direction of John Halkes, plays an increasingly useful role in the life of the community.

Few places in Cornwall have seen such postwar transformation as the Lizard peninsula. From the green fields outside Helston have flowered the helicopters of the Royal Naval Air Station of Culdrose, and from Goonhilly Downs have sprouted those spectacular 'dishes' of British Telecom International global satellite communications.

A photograph that looks almost like a painting from the Newlyn School. Waiting on the beach at Newlyn for the fish to arrive before the quays were built in the 1890s.

Just over twenty years ago Goonhilly became a pioneer in this science. By the end of the 1970s there were four aerials. Now there are seven, either built or under construction, including one for maritime work and one for lease satellite television.

In 1983 came the 21st anniversary of the opening of satellite communications, through Telstar, and there are still a half-a-dozen men working at the station who were there that day. It now links Britain with over eighty countries and I have a particular memory of one of those early historic events.

John Stonehouse came visiting as the Labour Government Minister responsible for this development, and spoke direct to Japan in opening the Indian Ocean satellite system. I recall him pacing up and down outside the station, making sure he was word-perfect for the occasion.

It holds some splendid records today. Goonhilly was the first to transmit colour television signals, the first to transmit by satellite a live television programme from Europe to America, and the first European earth station to make colour television transmissions from Australia and Canada. It is also a big employer...for there is a total staff of over two hundred.

The magical world. of modern communications did not begin and end at Poldhu, as I was reminded in 1979, when I watched Post Office experts land the shore end of their new telephone cable from Spain on Porthcurno beach.

Until the 1960s this remote corner of England was the country's centre of communication world-wide, with undersea cable links and networks that brought messages from Hong Kong, Singapore, the West Indies, Newfoundland, South Africa and South America to our shore and on to London.

It was here the first submarine telegraph cable across the Atlantic was brought ashore, and since then many others have been buried under the sands. Since 1970, however, Cable and Wireless Limited have not operated as a telegraph station, with satellites and other technology taking over, but their important role as a training college has continued.

When it was a world centre, led by Britain, it was natural that students should come and gain first-hand experience alongside an operational station. It must be hoped no move is made to leave the area, for it provides some seventy jobs, including the staff of twenty-four lecturers.

Once it was predominantly a British centre; today the bias is towards the overseas student with facilities for up to one hundred and fifty. As nations have become independent so they have wished to organise their own communications, and many come from the Arab world, from the West Indies, the Seychelles, Ceylon and India, even as far away as Cook Island and Macau to learn their skills.

The college dominates the village, but go a little way and you will find the gorgeous thick white sand of the beach, and then the Minack Theatre in the fractured granite.

The voice of Cornwall—*Above left*: Newlyn Male Choir in the old days—with the championship shield. *Below left*: Mousehole Male Voice Choir, with trophies, in the 1930s with conductor Mr Leonard Collins and accompanist Miss Humphreys. *Below*: Marazion 'Apollo' Male Voice Choir in its early days.

10

The View Ahead

I have written that the Bay is 'rich in its modern tapestry', but what is equally significant is that the tapestry remains incomplete, and that present and future generations will be contributing.

As the years pass there will be new heroes and heroines, fresh adventures, more battles to be fought and won.

The Cornish spirit will remain, whether by birth or by adoption. The words of that fine teacher Alan Wood, written for the former Humphry Davy Grammar School song, will ring as true to the next generation as they did to the last:

> As mighty waters ebb and flow
> Against our granite shore,
> So we, an ebbing tide, must go,
> This place be ours no more
> But other waves, from ocean deep
> Come surging in to land,
> Another race will take our place
> And bear the torch in hand

Acknowledgements

Mr John Farmer, the Cornwall County Librarian; Mr Terry Knight of the Local Studies Library, Redruth, and his staff; the Mayor of Penzance, Mrs Margaret Beckerleg; the Town Clerk of Penzance, Mr John Williams, the Town Council, and the Invigilator of the Penlee House Museum, Mr Brian Thomas; Mr Martin Matthews, Curator of the Helston Museum; the Penzance 'Morrab Gardens' Library; Mr John Corin; Mr H. L. Douch, Curator, and Mr R. D. Penhallurick, County Museum, Truro; the Editor of *The Cornishman*, Penzance; Mr Merville Matthews; Mrs Brenda Duxbury; Mrs Jane Williams; Mr T. C. Rising; British Telecom International; Royal Naval Air Station, Culdrose; Cable and Wireless Limited.

To the many men and women of West Cornwall who have told me of their experiences, and the many organisations that have contributed with information.

For assistance with photographs: Cornwall County Council, Penzance Town Council, Penlee House Museum, Morrab Library, County Museum, Truro, Helston Museum, Local Studies Library, Redruth, Messrs Sam Bennetts, David Woods, Andrew Besley, Frank Gibson, Robert Roskrow, George Waterhouse, Richard Bros, RNAS Culdrose, Mrs Pat Pilkerton, Dennis Jory, Jim Bottrell, Osborne Studios, Helston, Steve Hobden, Culdrose, Mobil, Mrs Enid Richards, Miss Margaret E. Bazeley and many others.

Photographs also included by the late Harry Penhaul and the late Tom Roskrow.

Bibliography: a selection

Bossiney Publications. **Cornish Shipwrecks** (Richard Larn and Clive Carter). **Wreck and Rescue Round the Cornish Coast** (Cyril Noall and Grahame Farr). **The King's England, Cornwall** (Arthur Mee). **Smuggling Days and Ways** (Capt. Henry N. Shore). **The Autobiography of a Cornish Smuggler** (Capt. Harry Carter). **The Book of Penzance** (Cyril Noall and Douglas Williams). **St Michael's Mount** (John St Aubyn).

Also Available

AROUND LAND'S END
Michael Williams explores the end and the beginning of Cornwall. Wrecks and legends, the Minack Theatre, Cable & Wireless, Penwith characters and customs, lighthouses and Lyonesse all feature. 90 photographs, many of them from Edwardian and Victorian times, help to tell the story.

THE CORNISH COUNTRYSIDE
by Sarah Foot. 130 illustrations, 40 in colour.
Words and pictures unite in presenting an evocative portrait of rich and varied landscapes.
'Sarah Foot sets out to share her obvious passion for Cornwall and to describe its enigmas ... It is a book for those who are already in love with Cornwall and for those who would like to know her better.'
Alison Foster, The Cornish Times

VIEWS OF OLD CORNWALL
by Sarah Foot.
Nearly 200 old picture postcards from the Peter Dryden collection, with text by Sarah Foot, all combine to recall Cornwall as she once was.
'...will be certain to start the talk flowing of days gone by.'
The Cornishman

CASTLES OF CORNWALL
by Mary and Hal Price. 78 photographs and map.
St Catherine's Castle and Castle Dore both at Fowey, Restormel near Lostwithiel, St Mawes, Pendennis at Falmouth, St Michael's Mount, Tintagel, Launceston and Trematon near Saltash. Mary and Hal Price on this tour of Cornwall explore these nine castles.
'...a lavishly illustrated narrative that is both historically sound and written in a compelling and vivid style that carries the reader along from one drama to the next.'
Pamela Leeds, The Western Evening Herald

THE CALL OF THE WEST
by Arthur Caddick
Selected lyric poems with a comic interlude.
'This book is as delightful as the reader can hope. The landscape, the seasons, the people, the history. Mr Caddick dips his lyric, his comic, his emotional pen—in turn—into the ink of life.
The Cornishman
'It's my belief that Arthur Caddick is the Dylan Thomas of Cornwall. Like Dylan Thomas he has the gift of touching our hearts.'
Derek Tangye

LEGENDS OF CORNWALL
by Sally Jones. 60 photographs and drawings.
Brilliantly illustrated with photographs and vivid drawings of legendary characters. A journey through the legendary sites of Cornwall, beginning at the Tamar and ending at Land's End.
'Highly readable and beautifully romantic...'
Desmond Lyons, Cornwall Courier

KING ARTHUR COUNTRY in CORNWALL
THE SEARCH for the REAL ARTHUR
by Brenda Duxbury, Michael Williams and Colin Wilson.
Over 50 photographs and 3 maps.
An exciting exploration of the Arthurian sites in Cornwall and Scilly, including the related legends of Tristan and Iseult, with The Search for the Real Arthur by Colin Wilson.
'...provides a refreshing slant on an old story linking it with the present.'
Caroline Righton, The Packet Newspapers

MY CORNWALL
A personal vision of Cornwall by eleven writers living and working in the county: Daphne du Maurier, Ronald Duncan, James Turner, Angela du Maurier, Jack Clemo, Denys Val Baker, Colin Wilson, C. C. Vyvyan, Arthur Caddick, Michael Williams and Derek Tangye, with reproductions of paintings by Margo Maeckelberghe and photographs by Bryan Russell.
'An ambitious collection of chapters.'
The Times, London

STRANGE HAPPENINGS IN CORNWALL
by Michael Williams. 35 photographs.
Strange shapes and strange characters; healing and life after death; reincarnation and Spiritualism; murders and mysteries are only some of the contents in this fascinating book.
'...this eerie Cornish collection.'
David Foot, Western Daily Press

THE CRUEL CORNISH SEA
by David Mudd. 65 photographs.
David Mudd selects more than 30 Cornish shipwrecks, spanning 400 years, in his fascinating account of seas at a coastline that each year claim their toll of human lives.
'This is an important book.'
Lord St Levan, the Cornish Times.

Other Bossiney Titles Include

A CORNISH CAMERA
by George Ellis and Sarah Foot.
More than 200 photographs taken by George Ellis, the doyen of Cornish press photographers: Cornwall at work and play in war and peace; town and countryside and coast; personalities and customs; triumphs and tragedies. Sarah Foot's text adds the stories behind these pictures.
'A delightful nostalgic look back at the last 40 years in the County.'
Sunday Independent

THE CORNISH YEAR BOOK
Over 150 photographs and drawings.
Writers, artists and photographers have all combined to reveal facets of Cornwall and a Cornish way of life through spring, summer, autumn and winter.

GHOSTS OF CORNWALL
by Peter Underwood. 41 drawings and photographs.
Peter Underwood, President of the Ghost Club, journeys across haunted Cornwall. Photographs of haunted sites and drawings of ghostly characters all combine to prove that Cornwall is indeed a mystic land.

SEA STORIES OF CORNWALL
by Ken Duxbury. 48 photographs.
'This is a tapestry of true tales' writes the author, 'by no means all of them disasters, which portray something of the spirit, the humour, the tragedy, and the enchantment, that is the lot of we who know the sea.'

HELSTON FLORA DAY
by Jill Newton. 48 photographs.
Jill Newton, with a combination of words and photographs, old and new, reflects some of that Flora Day music and magic.
'The text of this delightful little book is well supported with photographs old and new.'
Notes in the West, Western Morning News

OCCULT IN THE WEST
by Michael Williams. Over 30 photographs.
Michael Williams follows his successful **Supernatural in Cornwall** with further interviews and investigations into the Occult—this time incorporating Devon. Ghosts and clairvoyance, dreams and psychic painting, healing and hypnosis are only some of the facets of a fascinating story.
'...provides the doubters with much food for thought.'
Jean Kenzie, Tavistock Gazette

CURIOSITIES OF CORNWALL
by Michael Williams. 62 photographs.
Eccentric architecture; customs—curious, Cornish and Royal; curious characters and a curiosity that grew into invention and innovation; the deep hole at Delabole; the question witch or saint?...all these and much more prove that Cornwall has more than her share of curiosities.
'...a fascinating new book...avid collectors of offbeat gems of knowledge, whether they belong to the county or not, will welcome it as a treasure...'
Pamela Leeds, The Western Evening Herald

CORNISH MYSTERIES
by Michael Williams. 40 photographs.
Cornish Mysteries is a kind of jig-saw puzzle in words and pictures. The power of charming, mysterious shapes in the Cornish landscape, the baffling murder case of Mrs Hearn are just some fascinating ingredients.
'...superstitions, dreams, murder, Lyonesse, the legendary visit of the boy Jesus to Cornwall, and much else. Splendid, and sometimes eerie, chapters.'
The Methodist Recorder

VIEWS OF OLD DEVON
Rosemary Anne Lauder provides the text for more than 200 old postcards, evocative of a world and a way of life that has gone. Words and pictures combine to produce a book that will delight all who love Devon.
'Only the camera can turn back the clock like this.'
The Sunday Independent

VIEWS OF OLD PLYMOUTH
by Sarah Foot.
Words and old pictures combine to recall Plymouth as it once was: a reminder of those great times past and of the spirit of the people of Plymouth.
'This is a lovely nostalgia-ridden book and one which no real Plymothian will want to be without.'
James Mildren, The Western Morning News

We shall be pleased to send you our catalogue giving full details of our growing list of titles for Devon and Cornwall and forthcoming publications.

If you have difficulty in obtaining our titles, write direct to Bossiney Books, Land's End, St Teath, Bodmin, Cornwall.